Challenge Across America

by
Jerry Aten

illustrated by
Vanessa Filkins

Cover by Vanessa Filkins

Copyright © Good Apple, Inc., 1990

ISBN No. 0-86653-556-X

Printing No. 9876543

Good Apple, Inc.
1204 Buchanan St., Box 299
Carthage, IL 62321-0299

HOW TO PREPARE THE GAME...

The gameboard should be mounted on oaktag and either laminated or covered with Con-Tact paper to ensure its durability. It can also be mounted onto quarter-inch foam core. To do this, cut the foam core to the size of the playing area (24" x 35") with an X-acto knife and heavy ruler. Foam core can be purchased from any good art supply store. Mount the gameboard by carefully spraying an adhesive to back before positioning on the foam core.

Either laminate or cover with Con-Tact paper both the symbol and game question cards to give them a longer playing life. Then carefully cut on the dotted lines. The symbol cards can be placed at random in any size of box since students merely reach into the box, draw a card, identify the symbol and return the card to the box. The game cards should be stored in the storage box that can be created from the pattern on the back of the book cover or in a box of similar size that will allow the cards to be stacked for the convenience of the game monitor.

HOW TO PLAY...

The object of Challenge Across America is to travel the entire distance of one of the four paths across the gameboard before others who are playing the game. Moves along the various routes are accomplished by correctly answering the questions found on the game cards.

To begin, each player chooses the route he wishes to follow. All four paths have the same number of stops along the way. It becomes a simple matter of choice.

Each player charts his progress across the board with a coin or token that is different from those of other players. Players may choose to follow the same path others have chosen if they so desire.

A roll of the die will determine the order of play with the highest number rolled going first. To begin play, the first player draws one of the symbol cards from a box holding the cards. The symbol on the card chosen will determine the question the player will attempt to answer. Another player (or the teacher or game monitor) then draws a question card from the box containing the Challenge question cards and asks the question on the card that corresponds to the symbol drawn by the player answering the question.

If the player correctly answers the question, he then rolls the die and advances forward on his route the number of spaces equal to the number of spots showing on his roll of the die. Play then passes on to another player. If the player does not correctly answer his question, he is not allowed to roll the die and must remain in his current position on the board.

If a player lands on a red dot after rolling the die, he immediately earns the right to choose another symbol card and attempt to answer another question and earn the right to roll the die again and advance the proper number of spaces.

If a player chooses a symbol card that directs the game monitor to ask him a question with an asterisk and he correctly answers the question, he shall be entitled to two rolls of the die rather than the single roll awarded for answering other questions.

The first player to reach his destination at the end of his chosen route shall be considered the winner.

When a player nears the finish, he must roll a number on the die exactly needed to advance him to the finish line. If he gets within the last six spaces, he must first answer the question, then roll precisely the number of spaces needed to advance to the finish. For example, if a player's roll of the die takes him to within four spaces of the finish, to win the game, the player must correctly answer his question and then roll a four to win the game. If he fails at either of the above, play passes on to the next player.

GA1157

♣ This state has a panhandle in the extreme north that is less than fifty miles wide and is covered with Rocky Mountains that are a part of Kootenai National Forest. (Idaho)

✪ She founded Hull House in Chicago in 1889. (Jane Addams)

♦ Mt. Hood, the highest point in the state, is located in this western state. (Oregon)

✿ This city annually hosts the Miss America Pageant (Atlantic City, New Jersey)

☘ Our nation's gold reserves are stored here. (Fort Knox, Kentucky)

✪ The first capital of the Confederate States of America (Montgomery, Alabama)

♦ The capital of New Hampshire (Concord)

✿ Name the colors that appear on the signs that identify interstate highways across America. (Blue, red and white)

☘ Paducah, Bowling Green and Owensboro are here. (Kentucky)

✪ This lake serves as part of the boundary between Vermont and New York. (Lake Champlain)

♦ The Gem State (Idaho)

✿ The state that leads the nation in the production of automobiles (Michigan)

☘ Our most famous landmark, the Statue of Liberty, is located on an island next to this city. (New York City)

✪ This black scientist researched ways to make use of the peanut. (George Washington Carver)

♦ The capital city of Massachusetts (Boston)

✿ What patriotic organization uses the letters DAR? (Daughters of the American Revolution)

♣ The number of Spanish missions in California built between 1769 and 1823 to Christianize the Indians (21)

✪ The largest natural lake west of the Mississippi (Great Salt Lake)

♦ The Sunshine State (South Dakota or Florida)

✿ Which state capital is the highest above sea level? (Santa Fe, New Mexico, almost 7000 feet above sea level)

☘ Crater Lake National Park is located here. (Oregon)

✪ Name the professional baseball and football teams that call San Diego home. (Padres and Chargers)

♦ The capital city of California (Sacramento)

✿ He gave us the New Deal. (Franklin D. Roosevelt)

☘ John Adams, John Quincy Adams and John F. Kennedy were all gifts of this state to the U.S. presidency. (Massachusetts)

✪ Which first lady was a descendant of Pocahontas? (Edith Galt Wilson)

♦ The Bluegrass State (Kentucky)

✿ Which of our fifty states has the largest population? (California)

☘ South Carolina's contribution to the presidency (Andrew Jackson)

✪ There is only one U.S. coin that has the home of a former President embossed on it. Name the President and the name of his home. (Thomas Jefferson and Monticello)

♦ *The Chattahoochee National Forest and Okefenokee Swamp are both found here. (Georgia)

✿ He painted The Signing of the Constitution. (Louis S. Glanzman)

2

GA1157

♣ Its seven national forests include Wenatchee, Colville and Umatilla. (Washington)

★ The first woman to be elected a state governor (Nellie Tayloe Ross)

♦ Delaware and Pennsylvania are on the west; the Atlantic Ocean lies to the east. (New Jersey)

✿ The head judge of the Supreme Court is called Chief Justice. What are the other judges called? (Associate Justices)

♣ He served the shortest term of an elected President. (William Henry Harrison)

★ Martin Luther King, Bear Bryant and Helen Keller called this state home. (Alabama)

♦ *He discovered a glacier in Alaska, helped to establish Yosemite National Park, has a redwood forest named after him and founded the Sierra Club. (John Muir)

✿ Sandwiched between Idaho and Wyoming to the north and Arizona to the south (Utah)

♣ James Buchanan, Ben Franklin and Benjamin West are "products" of this eastern state. (Pennsylvania)

★ He was the "Father of the Constitution." (James Madison)

♦ Near what city is the U.S. Air Force Academy located? (Colorado Springs, Colorado)

✿ Seaford, Milford, Slaughter Beach and Wilmington are all found in this state. (Delaware)

♣ He said, "The only thing we have to fear is fear itself." (Franklin D. Roosevelt)

★ Roger Williams was this state's Founding Father. (Rhode Island)

♦ What is the President's title as head of the armed forces? (Commander-in-Chief)

✿ Disney World, Cypress Gardens, Sea World and Busch Gardens are all located here. (Florida)

♣ Abraham Lincoln was assassinated in this city. (Washington, D.C.)

★ He published the first American dictionary. (Noah Webster)

♦ This state is the nation's leading producer of gold. (Nevada)

✿ The cities of Bossier City, Kenner, Metairie and Shreveport are found in this southern state. (Louisiana)

♣ The largest of the contiguous United States (Texas)

★ It is called the "Mile High City." (Denver, Colorado)

♦ The Tar Heel State (North Carolina)

✿ The only President to be impeached (Andrew Johnson)

♣ This important river forms the eastern boundary of Nebraska. (Missouri)

★ Andrew Jackson's home in Nashville, Tennessee (The Hermitage)

♦ The state capital is Cheyenne. (Wyoming)

✿ He made the resolution that "these united colonies are, and of right ought to be, free . . . ." (Richard Henry Lee)

♣ Alaska's most important mineral (Oil)

★ The last major league baseball stadium to be equipped with lights (Wrigley Field in Chicago)

♦ Devil's Lake, Minot, Grand Forks and Jamestown are found here. (North Dakota)

✿ The only President inaugurated in New York City (George Washington)

3

GA1157

4

GA1157

- ♣ He sent American soldiers into South Korea. (Harry S. Truman)

- ★ The Volunteer State (Tennessee)

- ◆ This organization sponsors Boys State each year in all fifty states. (American Legion)

- ✿ The nation's number one producer of rice (Arkansas)

- ♣ Name two of the five Presidents who fought in the Civil War. (Grant, McKinley, Hayes, B. Harrison and Garfield)

- ★ This state leads the nation in the production of coal. (Kentucky)

- ◆ American statesman whose experiments proved that lightning is electricity. (Benjamin Franklin)

- ✿ Arches, Zion and Capitol Reef National Parks are located here. (Utah)

- ♣ The oldest road in the United States. It was first used in the late 1500's and runs from Santa Fe, New Mexico, to Chihuahua, Mexico. (El Camino Real)

- ★ It's called "Outdoor America" because it has the nation's oldest national park, national monument and national forest. (Wyoming)

- ◆ *Dwight D. Eisenhower defeated him twice for the U.S. presidency. (Adlai Stevenson)

- ✿ Kit Carson, Mamie Eisenhower, Gerald Ford and Peggy Fleming all called it home. (Colorado)

- ♣ *She wrote the poem inscribed on the Statue of Liberty. (Emma Lazarus)

- ★ To the east are South Carolina and the Atlantic; to the west, Alabama. (Georgia)

- ◆ What nickname was given to President Harding's friends whom he gave important jobs even though they weren't well qualified? (Ohio Gang)

- ✿ It is the smallest state west of the Appalachians except Hawaii, but it ranks twelfth in population. (Indiana)

- ♣ Swedish scientist who invented dynamite and later established monetary prize awards for those who achieve in various fields (Alfred Nobel)

- ★ The number one fish export in Washington (Salmon)

- ◆ The first Native American to befriend the Pilgrims (Squanto)

- ✿ Sandwiched between Nebraska on the north and Oklahoma on the south (Kansas)

- ♣ How many states were there in the Confederate States of America? (11)

- ★ This river serves as part of the boundary between Minnesota and Wisconsin. (Mississippi)

- ◆ He was the first President to die in office. (William Henry Harrison)

- ✿ To the west is Vermont; to the east lies Maine. (New Hampshire)

- ♣ The national park referred to as "The Alps of America" (Grand Teton)

- ★ The Rio Grande River flows right through the heart of the state from north to south and on to Mexico. (New Mexico)

- ◆ Who usually administers the oath of office to the President? (Chief Justice of the Supreme Court)

- ✿ The gambling capital of the East (Atlantic City, New Jersey)

- ♣ Into which Great Lake do the waters of all others flow? (Lake Ontario)

- ★ Myrtle Beach and Hilton Head are favorite vacation areas in this state. (South Carolina)

- ◆ George Washington's home in Virginia (Mount Vernon)

- ✿ Its professional baseball teams are called Rangers and Astros; its NFL football teams are called Cowboys and Oilers. (Texas)

GA1157

♣ What do the initials *TWA* stand for? (Trans World Airlines)

★ The Golden State (California)

◆ The British general who ended the Revolutionary War by surrendering Yorktown (Charles Cornwallis)

❀ Nebraska and Kansas are on the west; Illinois, Kentucky and Tennessee lie to the east. (Missouri)

☘ *Where did Lee and Grant meet to sign the terms of surrender that ended the Civil War? (Appomattox Court House, Virginia)

★ Minnesota is on the east; Montana on the west. (North Dakota)

◆ What was Mark Twain's real name? (Samuel L. Clemens)

❀ John Audubon, Truman Capote, Van Cliburn and Louis Armstrong all called this state home. (Louisiana)

☘ In what city did General Sherman's "March to the Sea" end? (Savannah, Georgia)

★ The only state with an oil well on the lawn of its capital (Oklahoma)

◆ During the War of 1812 this battle was fought two weeks after the war had ended. (Battle of New Orleans)

❀ To the north lie Colorado and Kansas; to the south is Texas. (Oklahoma)

☘ The only state whose borders touch four of the five Great Lakes (Michigan)

★ Decatur, Tuscaloosa and Montgomery are cities in this state. (Alabama)

◆ A Civil War battle fought between these two ships was the first involving ironclad ships. (*Monitor* and *Merrimack*)

❀ "Ike" was this state's favorite son. (Kansas)

☘ This mountain in Washington bears the same name as the highest mountain in Greece. (Mt. Olympus)

★ Arizona is on the west; Texas and Oklahoma are on the east. (New Mexico)

◆ Name the mountain range that extends from Canada into western Oregon and Washington and south into northern California. (Cascade Range)

❀ Shenandoah National Park is located here. (Virginia)

☘ Name America's three states that are peninsulas. (Alaska, Michigan and Florida)

★ Knott's Berry Farm, Yosemite National Park and Napa Valley are all here. (California)

◆ Name either of our two states with an Orange County. (Florida and California)

❀ Nebraska lies to the south; North Dakota lies to the north. (South Dakota)

☘ Former astronaut who became a U.S. senator and made a bid to become his party's candidate for President (John Glenn)

★ The "Heart of Dixie" (Alabama)

◆ The Buckingham Fountain is located in which U.S. city? (Chicago, Illinois)

❀ This state lies between Minnesota and Iowa on the west and Lake Michigan on the east. (Wisconsin)

☘ The tallest man-made monument in the United States (St. Louis Arch in Missouri)

★ Both the President of the Union and the Confederacy were born in this state. (Kentucky)

◆ The first major turnpike built in the United States (Pennsylvania Turnpike)

❀ The annual festival in New Orleans that precedes Lent (Mardi Gras)

GA1157

8

♣ A national park named after the river that runs through the park (Yellowstone National Park)

★ His is perhaps the best known rags-to-riches story in America. (Horatio Alger)

♦ The U.S. city with the greatest population of Chinese (San Francisco, California)

✿ The mighty Mississippi River has its modest beginning in this state. (Minnesota)

♣ He was the first vice president appointed to office. (Gerald Ford)

★ The capital city of Florida (Tallahassee)

♦ What long-lasting radio and television western used the "William Tell Overture" as its theme? (*Lone Ranger*)

✿ Andrew Jackson, James Polk and Andrew Johnson all distinguished themselves in this state. (Tennessee)

♣ Which U.S. President is depicted on a quarter? (George Washington)

★ To the west are California and Nevada; to the east is New Mexico. (Arizona)

♦ *He was the son of one President and the father of another. (John S. Harrison)

✿ This volcano in Washington erupted on May 18, 1980, leaving 150,000 acres of land devastated. (Mount St. Helens)

♣ This Mormon leader led his people to the Great Salt Lake in Utah. (Brigham Young)

★ To the north is New York; to the south, Delaware. (New Jersey)

♦ *The first U.S. woman to walk in space (Kathryn Sullivan)

✿ The "Penman of the American Revolution," John Dickinson, called this state home. (Delaware)

♣ Name the U.S. Commonwealth found in the Caribbean Sea. (Puerto Rico)

★ California's first highway (El Camino Real)

♦ The founder of the Mormon Church, he was murdered in Carthage, Illinois. (Joseph Smith)

✿ The Palmetto State (South Carolina)

♣ This state has the largest number of Amish people. (Pennsylvania)

★ To the north is Tennessee; to the south are Florida and the Gulf of Mexico. (Alabama)

♦ Plymouth, Massachusetts, was founded in 1620 by this group of people. (Pilgrims)

✿ Tongass National Forest and Misty Fiords National Monument are found in this state. (Alaska)

♣ What is the storied significance of Patrick and Catherine O'Leary's barn to the history of Chicago? (According to stories, this is where the Great Chicago Fire of 1871 started.)

★ The Sunflower State (Kansas)

♦ *The U.S. senator from Wisconsin who led the televised hearings investigating alleged communist influence in the U.S. Army (Joseph McCarthy)

✿ Bellingham, Spokane, Bellevue and Puyallup are cities here. (Washington)

♣ This poet and author was a noted authority on Abraham Lincoln. (Carl Sandburg)

★ The oldest seat of government in the United States (Santa Fe, New Mexico)

♦ How many members are there on the United Nations Security Council? (11)

✿ Grover Cleveland and Woodrow Wilson had ties with this state. (New Jersey)

9

GA1157

GA1157

♣ It is billed as the "Greatest Spectacle in Sports." (Indianapolis 500)

★ The United States imports more automobiles from this country than any other. (Japan)

♦ In 1793 this inventor revolutionized cotton cloth. (Eli Whitney)

✿ On which side of a speaker should the U.S. flag be displayed? (To the speaker's right on the platform, as he faces audience)

♣ The first black woman elected to the House of Representatives (Shirley Chisholm)

★ Hawaiian feast involving the roasting of a pig (Luau)

♦ Connecticut is on the west; Narragansett Bay is on the east. (Rhode Island)

✿ He was the first Roman Catholic to win an election for President. (John F. Kennedy)

♣ The Alamo, the Texas Ranger Hall of Fame and Astroworld are here. (Texas)

★ What do the letters *GOP* refer to in reference to the Republican party? (Grand Old Party)

♦ Duke University and Wake Forest (as well as the state university) are all prestigious universities located within a few miles of each other in this state. (North Carolina)

✿ The agency headed by J. Edgar Hoover for many years (FBI)

♣ The Cornhusker State (Nebraska)

★ In the game of baseball, what is meant by the term *southpaw*? (Left-handed pitcher)

♦ America's first national park (Yellowstone)

✿ This state is bordered by only one other state. (Maine)

♣ John Brown was hanged for his takeover of the U.S. Arsenal here. (Harpers Ferry now in West Virginia)

★ Under the Land Ordinance of 1785, how many acres were in a section of land? (640 or one square mile)

♦ Reading, Erie, State College and Altoona are all found here. (Pennsylvania)

✿ Name any three states that begin with *N*. (New Jersey, New Mexico, North Dakota, New York, Nebraska, North Carolina, Nevada and New Hampshire)

♣ Dartmouth College and the White Mountains are located here. (New Hampshire)

★ Which three states have land on the peninsula that is east of Chesapeake Bay? (Delaware, Maryland and Virginia)

♦ Canada lies to the north; Utah and Nevada are touching this state's southern border. (Idaho)

✿ The number of men who signed the Constitution (39)

♣ The Constitution State (Connecticut)

★ She was the first woman to earn a medical degree in the United States. (Elizabeth Blackwell)

♦ To the west is Utah; to the east lie Nebraska and Kansas. (Colorado)

✿ Name the song that is played when the President enters. ("Hail to the Chief")

♣ The historic James and Potomac Rivers flow through this state. (Virginia)

★ Name the first coeducational college in the United States. (Oberlin College in Ohio)

♦ The Battle of Coach's Bridge was the only conflict during the American Revolution fought on this state's soil. (Delaware)

✿ Name two of the three territories outside the U.S. whose residents are U.S. citizens. (Guam, Puerto Rico and the Virgin Islands)

11

GA1157

♣ Ft. Collins, Pueblo, Grand Junction and Durango are located here. (Colorado)

★ His election as President was decided by the House of Representatives because he was tied with another candidate in the Electoral College. (Thomas Jefferson)

◆ The southern border of this southern state is Florida; to the north lie Tennessee and North Carolina. (Georgia)

❀ This state leads the nation in the production of butter. (Wisconsin)

♣ National parks in this state are Mount Rainier, Cascades and Olympic. (Washington)

★ This state was the last to end Prohibition. (Mississippi)

◆ The name given to Boston's "walk through history" (Freedom Trail)

❀ What was the occupation of John Wilkes Booth, the accused assassin of Abraham Lincoln? (He was an actor.)

♣ Former Vice President Walter Mondale called this state home. (Minnesota)

★ Which state shares Niagara Falls with Canada? (New York)

◆ Washington and Oregon are on the west; Wyoming and Montana lie to the east. (Idaho)

❀ The Cotton Bowl is held in this city every year on New Year's Day. (Dallas, Texas)

♣ This river separates New Jersey from Pennsylvania. (Delaware)

★ It is the nation's largest art museum. (Metropolitan Museum of Art in New York City)

◆ Siuslaw and Willamette National Forests are located here. (Oregon)

❀ The only heavyweight boxing champion to retire without ever facing defeat ("Rocky" Marciano)

♣ The ethnic group of French Acadians who exiled from Canada to southern Louisiana in the 1700's (Cajuns)

★ What official document of citizenship is usually required in foreign countries? (Passport)

◆ The Ice Age Trail, St. Croix National Scenic Riverway and Nicolet National Forest are located here. (Wisconsin)

❀ The smallest of New York City's boroughs (Manhattan)

♣ The Show Me State (Missouri)

★ *He was the last President to be a slave owner. (Zachary Taylor)

◆ W.C. Handy, Harper Lee and George Washington Carver called this state home. (Alabama)

❀ *The name of the ship Sir Francis Drake sailed into Puget Sound in 1579 (*The Golden Hind*)

♣ Gallup, Los Alamos, Las Cruces and Roswell are cities here. (New Mexico)

★ The newest of our states (Hawaii)

◆ It was the home state of both Presidents named Roosevelt. (New York)

❀ Which first lady lived to the age of 96? (Bess Truman)

♣ Both Canyonlands and Bryce Canyon National Parks are located here. (Utah)

★ This city lays claim to both the 49'ers and the Giants. (San Francisco, California)

◆ The Platte River flows through the heart of this state. (Nebraska)

❀ When it is 5:00 a.m. in San Francisco, what time is it in Boston? (8:00 a.m.)

GA1157

14

GA1157

♣ To the south lie Mexico and the Gulf; to the north is Oklahoma. (Texas)

✪ Monterey Peninsula, Muir Woods and Death Valley are all found in this state. (California)

◆ What color is the granite out of which the Vietnam Veterans Memorial is molded? (Black)

❀ To the north is Canada; to the south is Massachusetts. (New Hampshire)

♣ Although its nickname is better known as something else, this state is sometimes called The Big Bend State because of a river bearing its name that bends sharply and flows through the state twice. (Tennessee)

✪ This agency protects the President and his family. (Secret Service)

◆ Jackson Hole, Cody, Thermopolis and Laramie are all located here. (Wyoming)

❀ It was at one time called the Nutmeg State. (Connecticut)

❀ This state has no other states touching its border. (Hawaii or Alaska)

✪ The state bird of Arkansas (Mockingbird)

◆ The name given to those who jumped the gun during the Oklahoma Land Rush. (Sooners)

❀ Denali, Katmai and Glacier Bay National Parks are all found here. (Alaska)

♣ The capital city in North Dakota (Bismarck)

✪ The nation's first subway was built in this city. (Boston, Massachusetts)

◆ Menlo Park, West Orange and Princeton are all located here. (New Jersey)

❀ The Columbia River is part of the northern boundary of this western state. (Oregon)

♣ The most coveted award in collegiate football (Heisman Memorial Trophy)

✪ It's bounded on the north by North Carolina, on the west by Georgia and on the east by the Atlantic Ocean. (South Carolina)

◆ This state has an Atlantic coastline, including Bethany Beach, Bowers Beach and the Bombay Hook National Wildlife Refuge Area. (Delaware)

❀ It is sometimes called the most northern of the southern states. (Florida)

♣ Hells Canyon, the deepest gorge in America, is located in this state. (Idaho)

✪ To the north is Utah; to the south is Mexico. (Arizona)

◆ In which cemetery can one visit the Tomb of the Unknown Soldier? (Arlington National Cemetery)

❀ The state capital of Arkansas (Little Rock)

♣ The capital city of Pennsylvania (Harrisburg)

✪ He dominated the steel industry during the late 1800's. (Andrew Carnegie)

◆ This presidential/vice-presidential team was nick-named Gritz & Fritz. (Jimmy Carter and Walter Mondale)

❀ Union General William Sherman burned this southern city in his famous march to the sea during the Civil War. (Atlanta, Georgia)

❀ Worcester, Salem and Brockton are all located here. (Massachusetts)

✪ Grand Portage and Pipestone are national monuments in this state. (Minnesota)

◆ Part of Great Smoky Mountains National Park is found on the western side of this state. (North Carolina)

❀ He is the only U.S. President to resign from office. (Richard Nixon)

15

GA1157

GA1157

♣ During pioneer days, what was Nebraska called? (The Great American Desert)

★ In which time zone is Denver, Colorado? (Mountain)

♦ This state hosts the world's largest outdoor rodeo. (Wyoming)

✿ This city plays host to the Orange Bowl. (Miami, Florida)

♣ To the east is Colorado; to the west is Nevada. (Utah)

★ Which of our fifty states lies closest to the equator? (Hawaii)

♦ The Battle of Chickamunga was fought in this state. (Tennessee)

✿ He assassinated Dr. Martin Luther King, Jr., in Memphis, Tennessee. (James Earl Ray)

♣ Bordered by Missouri to the north and Louisiana to the south (Arkansas)

★ This state has the largest coastline. (Alaska)

♦ The state where the bola tie originated and has been designated official neckware (Arizona)

✿ He was the youngest man to become a U.S. President at the age of 42. (Theodore Roosevelt)

♣ This city is called the "Pittsburgh of the South." (Birmingham, Alabama)

★ He was President of Mexico during the war with Mexico. (Santa Anna)

♦ The Crescent City (New Orleans, Louisiana)

✿ Name three of our state capitals that were named in honor of former Presidents. (Lincoln, NE; Jefferson City, MO; Jackson, MS and Madison, WI)

♣ Enid, Broken Arrow, Bartlesville and Muskogee are cities here. (Oklahoma)

★ For how long is a patent granted? (17 years)

♦ Independence, Missouri's most famous citizen (Harry S. Truman)

✿ *He started the tradition of having the President throw out the first ball to start the major league baseball season. (William H. Taft, 1910)

♣ The International Peace Garden lies on the border between the province of Manitoba in Canada and this state. (North Dakota)

★ The Smithsonian Institution is located here. (Washington, D.C.)

♦ The Ocean State (Rhode Island)

✿ He was President during the Spanish-American War. (William McKinley)

♣ The southernmost city in the contiguous United States (Key West, Florida)

★ It's awarded annually to the outstanding pitcher in each of the major leagues. (Cy Young Award)

♦ NASA, Kennedy Space Center's Spaceport and Everglades National Forest are here. (Florida)

✿ This one-word state has the most letters. (Massachusetts)

♣ The three points on the Triangle of History in Virginia (Yorktown, Jamestown and Williamsburg)

★ Name two of the five states carved out of the Northwest Territory. (Illinois, Indiana, Ohio, Michigan and Wisconsin)

♦ To the north is Pennsylvania; to the south lies Maryland. (Delaware)

✿ Name either of the lawyers who locked horns in the famous Scopes trial. (Clarence Darrow and William Jennings Bryan)

17

18

GA1157

✽ What is meant by the political term *lame duck*? (The time lapse of a defeated President between the election in November and the inauguration in January.)

★ The Prairie State (Illinois)

◆ America's number one producer of blueberries (Maine)

✽ This city is divided between Texas and Arkansas. (Texarkana)

♣ The second jewel of the Triple Crown in horse racing is run in Baltimore, Maryland. (Preakness)

★ His case wound up in the U.S. Supreme Court, where rules on the citizenship of slaves were redefined. (Dred Scott)

◆ The tallest mountain in the contiguous United States is in California. (Mt. Whitney)

✽ Our nation's deepest lake (Crater Lake)

♣ Louisiana and the Gulf of Mexico lie to the south; Tennessee is to the north. (Mississippi)

★ He wrote "The Midnight Ride of Paul Revere." (Henry Wadsworth Longfellow)

◆ Great Falls, Missoula and Butte are located here. (Montana)

✽ In the event that no candidate wins the proper majority in the Electoral College, who selects the vice president? (U.S. Senate)

♣ Second most important city in Nevada (Reno)

★ English explorer who discovered the Hawaiian Islands in 1778 (Captain James Cook)

◆ The surprise Japanese bombing here brought the United States into World War II. (Pearl Harbor)

✽ Name any of the rooms in the White House known by their color. (Green, blue and red)

✽ Burlington, Newport, St. Albans and Middleburg are located here. (Vermont)

★ He authorized dropping atomic bombs on Japan in World War II. (Harry S. Truman)

◆ The Hawkeye State (Iowa)

✽ Name four of the six flags that have flown over Texas. (Spain, France, Mexico, Republic of Texas, Confederate States and United States of America)

♣ To the south lie Indiana and Ohio; to the north is Canada. (Michigan)

★ Followed Rutherford B. Hayes as President (James Garfield)

◆ Cy Young, Harvey Firestone, Clarence Darrow and Annie Oakley all called this state home. (Ohio)

✽ What is the United States Military Academy commonly called? (West Point)

♣ This state is our nation's number one producer of apples. (Washington)

★ The breakfast cereal capital of the nation (Battle Creek, Michigan)

◆ Name the island on which the Statue of Liberty is located. (Liberty Island. Accept Bedloe's Island, its former name.)

✽ He assassinated President James A. Garfield. (Charles Guiteau)

♣ It served as a buffer in the 1700's to protect South Carolina colony from the Spanish in Florida. (Georgia)

★ This state produces more eggs than any other. (California)

◆ *The most populated county in the United States (Los Angeles County)

✽ This city on the Mississippi is called the "Gateway to the West." (St. Louis, Missouri)

GA1157

20

♣ Carpenters' Hall, The First Bank of the United States and the pavilion that houses the Liberty Bell are all found in this historic city. (Philadelphia, Pennsylvania)

✪ *The only reproduction of the Greek Parthenon is found in this U.S. city. (Nashville, Tennessee)

♦ The capital city of Wisconsin (Madison)

❀ It was the first state to secede from the Union. (South Carolina)

♣ Lakes Erie and Michigan lie to the north; West Virginia and Kentucky lie to the south. (Ohio)

✪ His assassination in 1968 was largely responsible for legislation providing for protection for presidential candidates. (Robert F. Kennedy)

♦ This river separates New Jersey from Delaware. (Delaware)

❀ Which decade experienced the Great Depression? (1930's)

♣ The First State (Delaware)

✪ The financial "street" of America (Wall Street)

♦ Massachusetts lies to the north; Block Island Sound is on the south. (Rhode Island)

❀ He proposed the League of Nations. (Woodrow Wilson)

♣ Its capital building is called "The Skyscraper on the Prairie." (North Dakota)

✪ In which state is Diamond Head? (Hawaii)

♦ The home state of Gerald and Henry Ford (Michigan)

❀ This symbol on the Great Seal of the United States stands for strength and self-reliance. (American eagle with shield)

♣ The capital city of Louisiana (Baton Rouge)

✪ It leads the nation in the growth of grapes. (California)

♦ The capital city of Iowa (Des Moines)

❀ The "hometown" of Tom Sawyer and Huckleberry Finn. (Hannibal, Missouri)

♣ Texas lies to the west, and Mississippi lies to the east. (Louisiana)

✪ Name the hill where the U.S. Capitol is located in Washington, D.C. (Capitol Hill)

♦ The city known as "The Big Apple" (New York City)

❀ To the east lies Georgia; to the west is Mississippi. (Alabama)

♣ How many members are there in both houses of Congress? (535)

✪ The Land of Opportunity (Arkansas)

♦ The Chisholm Trail connected these two towns. (San Antonio, Texas and Abilene, Kansas)

❀ The state capital of Vermont (Montpelier)

♣ This bird is the leading choice among state birds. (Cardinal or redbird)

✪ Both Tennessee and North Carolina share this national park. (Great Smoky Mountains)

♦ The length of a term of office for a U.S. senator (6 years)

❀ The state capital of Nebraska (Lincoln)

21

GA1157

22

GA1157

♣ The Hoosier State (Indiana)

★ This river in Idaho is the longest river that is found entirely within a single state. (Salmon)

♦ The capital city of Washington (Olympia)

♣ Name two of the three states with only five letters in their names. (Maine, Texas and Idaho)

♣ This popular country and western group bears the name of the state it calls home. (Alabama)

★ Which battle was considered the turning point of the Revolutionary War? (Saratoga)

♦ The capital city of Minnesota (St. Paul)

❀ It's known as the "Windy City." (Chicago, Illinois)

♣ This state is sandwiched between Arkansas and Louisiana on the west and Alabama on the east. (Mississippi)

★ This department is responsible for dealing with foreign embassies in the United States. (Department of State)

♦ This famous horse race is run on the first Saturday of every May. (Kentucky Derby)

❀ What historic landmark can be seen when one faces west atop the Washington Monument? (Lincoln Memorial)

♣ America's first woman astronaut in space (Sally Ride)

★ The Last Frontier (Alaska)

♦ It was the Confederate song of battle during the Civil War. ("Dixie")

❀ Name America's three largest states. (Alaska, Texas and California)

♣ What organization do the letters *OPEC* represent? (Organization of Petroleum Exporting Countries)

★ It was the first organized lawmaking body in the colonies. (Virginia House of Burgesses)

♦ New Hampshire lies to the west, the Atlantic Ocean to the east. (Maine)

❀ Three vice presidents have all had this last name. (Johnson: Richard, Andrew and Lyndon)

♣ The Beaver State (Oregon)

★ The longest continuous unarmed border between nations on earth (Border between the United States and Canada)

♦ Montana and Wyoming lie to the west; Iowa is on the east. (South Dakota)

❀ Thomas Jefferson's home (Monticello)

♣ Cape Hatteras, "The Graveyard of the Atlantic," has been set aside as a national seashore just off the coast of this state. (North Carolina)

★ How are former Presidents Richard Nixon and Dwight D. Eisenhower related? (Nixon's daughter, Julie, married David Eisenhower, grandson of Dwight D. Eisenhower)

♦ The world's tallest masonry structure (Washington Monument)

❀ The capital city of West Virginia (Charleston)

♣ The body of water that severs the port city of Baltimore (Chesapeake Bay)

★ Which state capital has the largest population? (Phoenix, Arizona, 1980 census)

♦ Twin Falls, Pocatello and Lewiston are cities here. (Idaho)

❀ *The title of the book by Bernstein and Woodward that related the true story of the Watergate scandal (*All the President's Men*)

23

GA1157

24

♣ He was President when the stock market crashed in October, 1929. (Herbert Hoover)

★ The Gopher State (Minnesota)

♦ *This Revolutionary war statue in Concord, Massachusetts, was the work of Daniel Chester French. (*The Minute Man*)

❀ The capital city of Missouri (Jefferson City)

♣ In Congress those who prefer war are called "Hawks." What are the congressmen called who prefer peace? (Doves)

★ The capital city in Oklahoma (Oklahoma City)

♦ In which direction would one travel to get from Salt Lake City to New York? (East)

❀ Arizona's state gem (Turquoise)

♣ He invented the game of basketball. (James Naismith)

★ The cities of Flagstaff, Snowflake and Yuma are located here. (Arizona)

♦ *These two gunslingers are buried next to each other in Boot Hill Cemetery in Deadwood, South Dakota. One is male, the other female. (Wild Bill Hickok and Calamity Jane)

❀ The cities of Provo, Ogden and Orem are located here. (Utah)

♣ Where is the headquarters of the United Nations? (New York City)

★ It's called the Equality State but is also known as the Cowboy State. (Wyoming)

♦ This Cooperstown, New York, citizen is credited as the founder of baseball. (Abner Doubleday)

❀ Name two of the three cities that hosted these Olympic Games: 1980, 1984, 1988. (1980 Moscow, 1984 Los Angeles, 1988 Seoul)

♣ This state's Latin derivative means "mountainous." (Montana)

★ She ran unsuccessfully with Walter Mondale in 1984. (Geraldine Ferraro)

♦ California is on the west; Utah and Arizona are on the east. (Nevada)

❀ The site of the second permanent English settlement in the Colonies (Plymouth, Massachusetts)

♣ The only state consisting entirely of islands (Hawaii)

★ The only person to serve as both President and vice president yet never elected as either (Gerald Ford)

♦ This state is sandwiched between New York and New Hampshire. (Vermont)

❀ What was the name used to describe the German mercenaries hired by the King of England during the Revolution? (Hessians)

♣ Maple syrup and granite are noted industries in this state. (Vermont)

★ The Erie Canal connects these two bodies of water. (Lake Erie and Hudson River)

♦ It's often called the "Land of Lincoln." (Illinois)

❀ He took the "giant leap for mankind," though it was but a small step for man. (Neil Armstrong)

♣ The state capital of Maine (Augusta)

★ *This President was the first to win a Nobel peace prize. (Theodore Roosevelt)

♦ To the west are West Virginia and Virginia; to the east is Delaware. (Maryland)

❀ The major river in Alaska that flows from east to west (Yukon)

25

GA1157

26

GA1157

♣ He said, "This is the place" when he saw the valley where Salt Lake City now stands. (Brigham Young)

★ Tupelo, Starkville, Hattiesburg and Meridian are cities here. (Mississippi)

♦ He was the first person to sign the U.S. Constitution. (George Washington)

❀ Missouri lies to the south; Minnesota lies to the north. (Iowa)

☘ This state has the largest number of representatives in the House. (California)

★ The Great Lake State (Michigan)

♦ She was nicknamed "Moses" for her role in the Underground Railroad. (Harriet Tubman)

❀ This state lies between Nebraska and South Dakota on the west and Wisconsin and Illinois on the east. (Iowa)

♣ This U.S. President was called "Little Ben." (Benjamin Harrison)

★ The Lone Star State (Texas)

♦ This nuclear power plant in Pennsylvania malfunctioned in 1979 causing a dangerous radiation leak into the atmosphere. (Three Mile Island)

❀ To the west is Tennessee; to the east lies the Atlantic. (North Carolina)

♣ How many rows of horizontal stars are there on the U.S. flag? (9)

★ Wild Bill Hickok was hired to restore law and order to this town. (Dodge City, Kansas)

♦ She was the Indian guide of Lewis and Clark during their historic journey. (Sacajawea)

❀ This state is sandwiched between British Columbia and Oregon. (Washington)

♣ Which state has *Big Sky* printed on its license plates? (Montana)

★ *This U.S. President wore a pince-nez. (Theodore Roosevelt)

♦ The state in which Hot Springs National Park is located. (Arkansas)

❀ What is the Statue of Liberty holding in her right hand? (Torch)

☘ The Grand Canyon State (Arizona)

★ What nickname did Southerners call Northerners during the Civil War? (Yankees)

♦ The Black Hills spruce is the state tree. (South Dakota)

❀ What name is used to describe the mining towns in the "early west" that sprang up quickly and were then abandoned? (Ghost towns)

♣ This southeastern state ranks second only to California in peaches. (South Carolina)

★ Which state borders a Canadian territory? (Alaska)

♦ To the north is Arkansas and to the south is the Gulf of Mexico. (Louisiana)

❀ More Presidents (6) have had this first name than any other. (James)

♣ The Sooner State (Oklahoma)

★ How many soldiers were buried in the Tomb of the Unknown Soldier? (4)

♦ The capital city of Utah (Salt Lake City)

❀ Manhattan Island is one of the three islands on which much of New York City stands. Name one of these other two islands. (Long Island and Staten Island)

27

28

♣ Name the historical incident that occurred on December 16, 1773, when three shiploads of tea were dumped into the Boston Harbor. (Boston Tea Party)

✪ Beale Street, known as the "Birth of the Blues," is located in this Tennessee city. (Memphis, Tennessee)

◆ What is the significance of 1600 Pennsylvania Avenue? (The address of the White House)

❀ The capital city of Indiana (Indianapolis)

♣ Which state capital is named after a large pole used by Indians for animal sacrifices? (Baton Rouge, Louisiana)

✪ Peter Minuit established a small Swedish settlement in what would later become part of this state in 1638. (Delaware)

◆ This state has a coastline on both the Atlantic Ocean and the Gulf of Mexico. (Florida)

❀ The Granite State (New Hampshire)

♣ Which three states have only four letters in their spellings? (Utah, Ohio and Iowa)

✪ The Peach State (Georgia)

◆ It was the first written plan for self-government in America. (Mayflower Compact)

❀ Green Bay, Baraboo, Eau Claire and Oshkosh are all located here. (Wisconsin)

♣ What is the origin of the Louisiana word *Cajun*? (From Acadians—Louisiana settlers who came there after being driven out of Nova Scotia)

✪ The capital city of Alaska (Juneau)

◆ Both the Oregon Trail and the Old Santa Fe Trail started in this city. (Kansas City, Missouri)

❀ To the south is North Carolina; to the north are West Virginia and Maryland. (Virginia)

♣ Name either of the two states that share borders with more states than any other. (Tennessee and Missouri)

✪ Chief Joseph surrendered his fight against the white man ending the Nez Perce War in this state. (Idaho)

◆ This state leads all others in the production of oil. (Texas)

❀ The capital city of Rhode Island (Providence)

♣ She organized the American Red Cross. (Clara Barton)

✪ Lakeland, Panama City, Daytona Beach and Gainesville are all found in this state. (Florida)

◆ What were the two primary metals found in the Comstock Lode? (Gold and silver)

❀ It's bounded on the north by the Ohio River and on the south by Tennessee. (Kentucky)

♣ This song was played as the British troops surrendered their arms at Yorktown. ("The World Turned Upside Down")

✪ To the north are Vermont and New Hampshire; to the south Connecticut and Rhode Island. (Massachusetts)

◆ What do the letters *USS* stand for in reference to naval vessels? (United States Ship)

❀ The only state with a unicameral state legislature (Nebraska)

♣ Which state has both the youngest average population and the coolest temperature average? (Alaska)

✪ It boasts the nation's greatest drop of any ski area. (Wyoming)

◆ What is the significance of Cooperstown, New York, to major league baseball players? (The Baseball Hall of Fame is located there.)

❀ Colorado lies to the north, Texas and Mexico to the south. (New Mexico)

29

GA1157

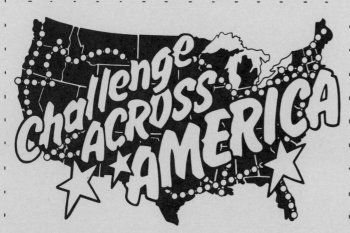 

♣ Walter Lenox, Thomas Edison and John D. Rockefeller all did much of their work in this state. (New Jersey)

✪ What was the name of the publication started by Benjamin Franklin in 1732 that was filled with humor and advice and highly popular? (*Poor Richard* or accept *Poor Richard's Almanac*)

♦ Six Flags over Mid-America, Silver Dollar City and Lake of the Ozarks are the main tourist attractions in this state. (Missouri)

❀ Name the first billion dollar corporation in the United States. (U.S. Steel)

♣ To the north lies Canada; to the south lies South Dakota. (North Dakota)

✪ To whom did the term *Founding Fathers* refer? (Those who attended the Constitutional Convention)

♦ The state capital of New York (Albany)

❀ What was the face value of the eagle gold coin? ($10)

♣ Eugene, Coos Bay, Pendleton and Salem are all located here. (Oregon)

✪ Which city's freeway system handles more vehicles per day than any other? (Los Angeles, California)

♦ The capital city of Connecticut (Hartford)

❀ What was the law passed in 1850 that helped to enforce earlier laws dealing with runaway slaves? (Fugitive Slave Law Act)

♣ Rocky Mountain National Park is located here. (Colorado)

✪ He was a hero in the Spanish-American War and would later become President. (Theodore Roosevelt)

♦ Pennsylvania lies to the north of this state, Virginia to the south. (West Virginia)

❀ From what continent were the first inhabitants of North America thought to have come? (Asia)

♣ The Keystone State (Pennsylvania)

✪ Which father and son both became Presidents of the United States? (John Adams and John Quincy Adams)

♦ Big Bend and Guadalupe Mountains are national parks in this state. (Texas)

❀ The nickname for the area in California where computer chips and computer technology enjoy their finest hour (Silicon Valley)

♣ Both the firefly and the ladybug are official insects of this southern state. (Texas)

✪ What is the largest denomination of U.S. currency? ($100,000 bill)

♦ The capital city of Georgia (Atlanta)

❀ On what body of water is the city of Galveston located? (Gulf of Mexico)

♣ The Wabash River forms part of its western boundary; the Ohio River is its southern boundary. (Indiana)

✪ In what city is the Vietnam Veterans Memorial located? (Washington, D.C.)

♦ Huntington, Beckley, Clarksburg and Morgantown are all cities in this state. (West Virginia)

❀ In which U.S. city does one go to see "Old Ironsides" today? (Boston, Massachusetts)

♣ To the west are West Virginia and Ohio; to the east are New Jersey and New York. (Pennsylvania)

✪ A picture of King Kamehameha is found on license plates in this state. (Hawaii)

♦ The Badger State (Wisconsin)

❀ Name the three major bodies of salt water that touch the borders of the contiguous United States. (Atlantic Ocean, Pacific Ocean and Gulf of Mexico)

GA1157

32

GA1157

♣ Aspen, one of America's most popular ski resorts, is located here. (Colorado)

✪ Who was the losing candidate in the election for President in 1976? (Gerald Ford)

◆ The Empire State (New York)

❀ This President founded the National Foundation for Infantile Paralysis because he himself had been afflicted. (Franklin D. Roosevelt)

♣ The Land of Enchantment (New Mexico)

✪ Who follows the vice president in the line of succession to the presidency? (Speaker of the House)

◆ To the east are Nevada and Arizona; to the west is the Pacific Ocean. (California)

❀ This southern state leads the nation in the production of chickens. (Georgia)

♣ The Missouri River cuts through this state diagonally from north to south, separating the Great Plains from the Midwest. (South Dakota)

✪ Name three of the four states that touch Lake Erie. (New York, Ohio, Michigan and Pennsylvania)

◆ This state leads the nation in the production of cotton. (Texas)

❀ In what city is Steinbeck's Cannery Row located? (Monterey, California)

♣ This wild Idaho river is often referred to as "The River of No Return." (Salmon)

✪ He wrote the highly popular American Spelling Book in 1783. (Noah Webster)

◆ The Golden Gate Bridge is one of San Francisco's most famous landmarks. What color is it? (Orange)

❀ He was our nation's first Secretary of the Treasury. (Alexander Hamilton)

♣ The Dutch called this city New Amsterdam. Today it's known by another name. (New York City)

✪ What act of Congress was passed in 1862 giving free land to settlers on the Great Plains? (Homestead Act)

◆ To the west is New Mexico; to the east are Missouri and Arkansas. (Oklahoma)

❀ Abraham Lincoln and Stephen Douglas were competing for this office when they staged their famous series of debates. (U.S. senator)

♣ Salina, Great Bend, Hutchinson and Emporia are cities here. (Kansas)

✪ In this building began the downfall of Richard Nixon. (Watergate)

◆ The steel plants along this state's northwestern area near Lake Michigan make this one of the heaviest industrial areas. (Indiana)

❀ Name the first major land acquisition purchased by the United States. (Louisiana Territory)

♣ This Minnesota port city is the westernmost in the Great Lakes System. (Duluth)

✪ Even though he wasn't President, his portrait is found on a $100 bill. (Benjamin Franklin)

◆ The Mountain State (West Virginia)

❀ The license plates on cars in this state have the words Green Mountains printed on them. (Vermont)

♣ Allegheny National Forest is the only national forest found in this eastern state that has over half its land covered by forests. (Pennsylvania)

✪ This mountain range is a part of the Rocky Mountains located along the Idaho-Montana border. (Bitterroot)

◆ It's often called "America's Dairyland," as it leads the nation in the production of dairy products. (Wisconsin)

❀ These port cities—Seattle, Olympia and Tacoma—are found on what body of water? (Puget Sound)

GA1157

34

♣ Prudhoe Bay, the Yukon River and Norton Sound are found here. (Alaska)

★ It is the second most often spoken language in the United States. (Spanish)

♦ Maryland is on the west, and just across the river to the east is New Jersey. (Delaware)

❀ America's longest river (Mississippi)

♣ Lynchburg, Staunton, Alexandria and Colonial Heights are cities here. (Virginia)

★ This early policy promised U.S. protection of Latin American countries from ambitious European takeover. (Monroe Doctrine)

♦ Where would a "midshipman" go to school? (U.S. Naval Academy)

❀ This lawyer, who would later become President, helped to defend the British soldiers involved in the Boston Massacre. (John Adams)

♣ Pawtucket, Bristol and Warwick are located here. (Rhode Island)

★ This state leads the nation in artichokes. (California)

♦ To the west of this state lie the states of Kentucky and Ohio; to the east is Virginia. (West Virginia)

❀ This river flows through the Grand Canyon. (Colorado)

♣ Gerald R. Ford, our 38th President, was born in this state. (Nebraska)

★ He started the first mail-order company in Chicago in the 1870's. (Montgomery Ward)

♦ To the north lies Virginia; to the south are Georgia and South Carolina. (North Carolina)

❀ On which foot is the Statue of Liberty placing the most weight? (Left foot. The right foot is behind and appears to be used for balance.)

♣ This state has the Theodore Roosevelt National Park within its boundaries. (North Dakota)

★ The words *Peace Garden State* are printed on the license plates of this state. (North Dakota)

♦ He was governor of Plymouth colony of Pilgrims from 1620 until his death. (William Bradford)

❀ He wrote the Declaration of Independence. (Thomas Jefferson)

♣ To the north lies Washington. Nevada and California lie to the south. (Oregon)

★ It is sometimes called the "City of Fountains" because it has more fountains than any other city in the United States. (Kansas City, Missouri)

♦ Which building in Washington, D.C., serves as the site of the inauguration of Presidents? (Capitol)

❀ The city in the United States that is farther east than any other (Eastport, Maine)

♣ The capital city of Idaho (Boise)

★ In which city is NASA's Mission Control Center? (Houston, Texas)

♦ To the east are Virginia and West Virginia, to the west, Illinois and Missouri. (Kentucky)

❀ This state has the word *Wander* on its license plates. (Indiana)

♣ The Bay State (Massachusetts)

★ He became President in 1912 when Theodore Roosevelt stepped in and split the Republican vote. (Woodrow Wilson)

♦ It includes Badlands National Park and Mount Rushmore National Memorial. (South Dakota)

❀ He organized the United Mine Workers. (John L. Lewis)

GA1157

♣ Its oldest city is Charleston. (South Carolina)

★ Of the states with two words in their names, only this one has two words in its capital city. (Santa Fe, New Mexico)

♦ The capital city of Alabama (Montgomery)

❀ This area of Washington, D.C., NW, is a vibrant hub of nightclubs, restaurants, specialty shops and restored homes. (Georgetown)

♣ Natural Bridges and Dinosaur National Monuments are located in this state. (Utah)

★ What is the money called that is deposited with the court to gain temporary release of the accused and to guarantee appearance in court? (Bail)

♦ This state is sandwiched between North and South Dakota on the west and Lake Superior and Wisconsin on the east. (Minnesota)

❀ How many sections were contained in a township under the rules established by the U.S. Land Ordinance of 1785? (36)

♣ Lewis and Clark began their famous trek to the northwest from this city. (St. Louis, Missouri)

★ The only state where the flowering dogwood is both the state tree and state flower (Virginia)

♦ Name the five boroughs of New York City. (Queens, Brooklyn, Bronx, Manhattan and Richmond)

❀ *He was in charge of the U.S. troops in South Vietnam from 1964-1968. (General William Westmoreland)

♣ This state is bound on the east and west by Idaho and the Pacific Ocean. (Oregon)

★ The number of men who signed the Declaration of Independence (56)

♦ To the north lies Oregon; to the south is Mexico. (California)

❀ His campaign slogan was "A chicken in every pot, a car in every garage." (Herbert Hoover)

♣ The Pelican State (Louisiana)

★ On what date is the inauguration of the President usually held? (January 20)

♦ The five civilized tribes were relocated here from their tribal homes in the East. (Oklahoma)

❀ Which of the contiguous United States extends farthest north? (Minnesota)

♣ The name of this state is a French version of a Chippewa Indian word that means "gathering of waters." (Wisconsin)

★ Name any of the three men who wrote the Federalist Papers. (John Jay, James Madison and Alexander Hamilton)

♦ The highest mountain peak in North America (Mt. McKinley)

❀ Out of what kind of rock were the four faces of Mount Rushmore carved? (Granite)

♣ The state which has the most native Indians (Arizona)

★ He broke Babe Ruth's career home run record. (Henry Aaron)

♦ It was the home of Yankee Peddlers. (Connecticut)

❀ Name three of the four states that share the shores of Lake Michigan. (Wisconsin, Indiana, Illinois and Michigan)

♣ Deadwood and Korczak Ziolkowski's unfinished tribute to Crazy Horse are located here. (South Dakota)

★ She was the first woman pilot to fly from Hawaii to the mainland of the United States. (Amelia Earhart)

♦ The capital city of Virginia (Richmond)

❀ What is the historical significance of August 8, 1974? (It is the date Richard Nixon announced his resignation as President.)

GA1157

38

- ♣ This prestigious Ivy League school in Providence, Rhode Island, is America's seventh oldest university. (Brown)

- ✪ Where was the second capital of the Confederacy? (Richmond, Virginia)

- ♦ What state once called itself Kanawha? (West Virginia)

- ❀ The neighborhood in Washington, D.C., where many of the 150 foreign embassies are located. (Embassy Row)

- ♣ To the north is Michigan; to the south is Kentucky. (Indiana)

- ✪ He chose the front of the Lincoln Memorial to deliver his famous "I Have a Dream" speech. (Martin Luther King, Jr.)

- ♦ The number one cash crop in Kansas (Wheat)

- ❀ Name four of the eight vice presidents later elected President. (Adams, Jefferson, T. Roosevelt, Coolidge, Truman, Nixon, L. Johnson and Bush)

- ♣ Mammoth Cave National Park is located here. (Kentucky)

- ✪ This city annually hosts the Rose Bowl. (Pasadena, California)

- ♦ The nation's first kindergarten was started in this state noted as a leader in education. (Wisconsin)

- ❀ This ship brought the Pilgrims to Plymouth Rock in 1620. (*Mayflower*)

- ♣ Our largest state, it also has the fewest number of people. (Alaska)

- ✪ The name used to refer to the patriots who were prepared to fight the British at a "minute's" notice (Minutemen)

- ♦ This state was created by Congress as a result of its loyalty to the Union during the Civil War. (West Virginia)

- ❀ What was Hoover Dam called before it was named Hoover Dam? (Boulder Dam)

- ♣ To the north lie Lake Erie and the state of New York; to the south are West Virginia and Maryland. (Pennsylvania)

- ✪ *During the War of 1812 he said, "We have met the enemy and they are ours." (Oliver Hazard Perry)

- ♦ To the east are the states of Louisiana and Arkansas; to the west is New Mexico. (Texas)

- ❀ America's first of many "theme parks" located in Anaheim, California (Disneyland)

- ♣ Winston-Salem, Greensboro, Asheville and Greenville are cities in this state. (North Carolina)

- ✪ He was called "Old Hickory." (Andrew Jackson)

- ♦ Sioux Falls, Rapid City, Keystone and Mitchell are located here. (South Dakota)

- ❀ This state leads the nation in the production of packed sardines. (Maine)

- ♣ John Calhoun was born in Abbeville in this southern state. (South Carolina)

- ✪ Name the two American capitals that have been occupied by enemy forces. (Philadelphia and Washington)

- ♦ South Carolina's state capital (Columbia)

- ❀ Name America's only five-star general to become President. (Dwight D. Eisenhower)

- ♣ The U.S. battleship sunk by the Japanese in Pearl Harbor in which over 1700 men lost their lives (*USS Arizona*)

- ✪ Which President was a former movie star? (Ronald Reagan)

- ♦ Abilene, Galveston, Corpus Christi and Brownsville are all cities in this state. (Texas)

- ❀ America's first black astronaut to orbit the earth (Guion Bluford)

GA1157

40

♣ German scientist who helped launch the Apollo Moon Missions for NASA (Wernher von Braun)

✪ This Massachusetts city has been nicknamed the Hub. (Boston)

♦ Which of the Great Lakes is not shared with Canada but lies entirely within the border of the United States? (Lake Michigan)

❀ Rochester, Saint Cloud, Duluth and Mankato are cities in this state. (Minnesota)

♣ He was President when U.S. troops were withdrawn from South Vietnam. (Richard Nixon)

✪ Its boundary includes the three southernmost offshore Isles of Shoals. (New Hampshire)

♦ The only President to serve two nonconsecutive terms (Grover Cleveland)

❀ The Garden State (New Jersey)

♣ His portrait is found on a $50 bill. (Ulysses S. Grant)

✪ It was the home state of these celebrities: Gene Sarazen, Arthur Miller, Sugar Ray Robinson. (New York)

♦ This river forms part of the boundary between Kansas and Missouri. (Missouri)

❀ He discovered Florida while searching for the mythical Fountain of Youth. (Ponce de Léon)

♣ Wailuku, Hilo, Waipahu and Kahului are cities here. (Hawaii)

✪ The nickname of the USS Constitution ("Old Ironside")

♦ The Silver State (Nevada)

❀ It is the largest of the Great Lakes. (Lake Superior)

♣ This state lies between Idaho on the west and North Dakota on the east. (Montana)

✪ He said, "I only regret that I have but one life to lose for my country." (Nathan Hale)

♦ This expanse of California lies between the North American Plate and the Pacific Plate. (San Andreas Fault)

❀ Julien Dubuque was the first white settler in this state. (Iowa)

♣ Talladega National Forest, the Chattahoochee River and Tuskegee Institute are here. (Alabama)

✪ Name the two state capitals that include the names of their states. (Oklahoma City and Indianapolis)

♦ The Centennial State (Colorado)

❀ Which comes closest to the length of the border between the United States and Canada? 2000 miles, 3000 miles, 4000 miles? (4000 miles)

♣ Bloomington, Cairo, Peoria and Decatur are cities here. (Illinois)

✪ Name the three contiguous states that have a Pacific coastline. (Washington, Oregon and California)

♦ This state's nickname is "Old Dominion." (Virginia)

❀ Famous pioneer "trailblazer" who helped build the Wilderness Road between Virginia and Kentucky (Daniel Boone)

♣ To the north is the Canadian border; to the south lies Iowa. (Minnesota)

✪ He is called the "Father of the Navy." (John Paul Jones)

♦ The birthplace of the United States Navy (Newport, Rhode Island)

❀ This humorist/author who was born on the year of Halley's Comet passing the earth predicted he would die the next time it came and he did. (Samuel Clemens, Mark Twain)

GA1157

42

GA1157

♣ In which state is the geographic center of the United States? (Kansas)

✪ Both Dollywood and Opryland are located in this state. (Tennessee)

♦ This agency under the Department of Transportation monitors the safety of all aircraft. (Federal Aviation Authority)

❀ How many turns would one make to walk around the Pentagon? (5)

♣ The significance of tiny Plains, Georgia, to American history (The home of the 39th U.S. President, Jimmy Carter)

✪ Female desperado who consorted with such notorious outlaws as Jesse James and Cole Younger (Belle Starr)

♦ *The canals and locks that connect Lake Erie and Lake Ontario (Welland Ship)

❀ Name five of the six New England states. (Massachusetts, New Hampshire, Vermont, Connecticut, Maine and Rhode Island)

♣ This state is referred to as the "Mother of Presidents." (Virginia)

✪ The term *antebellum* refers to the time prior to what period in American history? (Civil War)

♦ He patented the kinetoscope camera which later led to motion pictures. (Thomas Edison)

❀ The term used for the correct positioning of the American flag during periods of national mourning (Half-mast)

❀ She was a movie actress until she married Prince Rainier II of Monaco. (Grace Kelly)

✪ The George Washington National Forest and Skyline Drive along the top of the Blue Ridge Mountains are here. (Virginia)

♦ In 1929 he was making more money for hitting home runs than Herbert Hoover was making for being President. (Babe Ruth)

❀ The historic significance of Kitty Hawk, North Carolina (It was the site of the famous "first flight" of Wilbur and Orville Wright.)

♣ According to the census of 1980, the population center of the United States (the same number of people to the east as to the west and the same number to the north as to the south) is now located in this state. (Missouri)

✪ The capital city of Delaware (Dover)

♦ He was the first black justice on the U.S. Supreme Court. (Thurgood Marshall)

❀ His picture is on a $10 bill. (Alexander Hamilton)

♣ This fort located in Charleston, South Carolina, was attacked by Confederate soldiers on April 12, 1861, and started the Civil War. (Fort Sumter)

✪ The largest river in Alaska (Yukon)

♦ Fort Sill, Chickasaw National Recreation Area and the National Cowboy Hall of Fame are here. (Oklahoma)

❀ During this war the concept of Daylight Saving Time was introduced to conserve energy. (World War I)

♣ Lombard Street, billed as the "Crookedest Street in America," is located in this city. (San Francisco, California)

✪ His face is the only one of the four carved on Mount Rushmore wearing glasses. (Theodore Roosevelt)

♦ The maximum length of time a person can be President of the United States (10 years)

❀ Our oldest national monument (Devils Tower)

❀ He was President Lincoln's first choice to lead the Union Army. (Robert E. Lee. But he declined because of his loyalty to Virginia and the South)

✪ This state has the outline of a peninsula on its license plate. (Florida)

♦ He led the first expedition to the North Pole. (Admiral Robert E. Peary)

❀ Greenville, Darlington, Georgetown, Spartanburg and Charleston are all in this state. (South Carolina)

GA1157

44

GA1157

♣ He uses *Air Force Two*. (Vice president)

✪ In 1854 he was instrumental in establishing U.S. relations with Japan. (Commodore Matthew Perry)

♦ The capital city is Pierre. (South Dakota)

❀ The religious denomination in the United States with the most members (Roman Catholic Church)

♣ The largest city on the Great Lakes (Chicago, Illinois)

✪ The city known as the "Cradle of Liberty" (Boston, Massachusetts)

♦ The name of the first man-made satellite launched by Russia in 1957 (*Sputnik I*)

❀ Name the day traditionally set aside for planting trees. (Arbor Day)

♣ He was shot and killed in a pistol dual by Aaron Burr in 1804. (Alexander Hamilton)

✪ The state in which both the Ozark and Ouachita Mountains are located (Arkansas)

♦ Name the agricultural crop for which George Washington Carver developed the greatest number of uses. (Peanut)

❀ To the nearest mile, what is the distance of a marathon? (26 miles)

♣ This southern city hosted the 1984 World's Fair. (New Orleans, Louisiana)

✪ On September 11, 1985, he broke Ty Cobb's long-standing record of 4190 lifetime hits. (Pete Rose)

♦ Missouri lies to the east and Colorado to the west. (Kansas)

❀ This famous American was born on February 12, 1809. (Abraham Lincoln)

♣ This river lies between Texas and Mexico. (Rio Grande)

✪ He shot and killed the accused assassin of John F. Kennedy. (Jack Ruby)

♦ What were the pioneers of America making reference to when they spoke of the "Great American Desert"? (The Great Plains)

❀ The largest desert in the United States (Mojave)

♣ Mt. St. Helens, Mt. Rainier and Mt. Hood are a part of this mountain range. (Cascade Mountains)

✪ The home state of American humorist Will Rogers (Oklahoma)

♦ Jackson's Mill, the National Radio Astronomy Observatory and the Greenbrier River are attractions for tourists in this state. (West Virginia)

❀ *The only U.S. President with a Ph.D. (Woodrow Wilson)

♣ What cities are identified with Disneyland and Disney World? (Anaheim, California and Orlando, Florida)

✪ *Her book entitled *Etiquette* was the first to have a strong influence on manners in America. (Emily Post)

♦ This state was the stage for the Lincoln-Douglas debates of 1858. (Illinois)

❀ America's longest land tunnel that handles moving vehicles (Eisenhower Memorial Tunnel in Colorado)

♣ The only President to have a last name made up of two words (Martin Van Buren)

✪ What was the nickname identified with the decade of the 1920's? (Roaring Twenties)

♦ This state capital has three words. (Salt Lake City)

❀ The agency of the federal government that licenses radio and television stations (Federal Communications Commission)

GA1157

46

GA1157

♣ What do the initials *D.C.* stand for in Washington, D.C.? (District of Columbia)

★ This port city handles more tonnage per year than any other in the United States. (New Orleans, Louisiana)

♦ Which European country gave the Statue of Liberty to the United States as a present? (France)

❀ To the north is Canada; to the south lie Pennsylvania, New Jersey and Connecticut. (New York)

♣ This city hosts the Kentucky Derby each year in May. (Louisville, Kentucky)

★ What is the minimum age requirement for a U.S. President? (35)

♦ It was used by pioneers as fuel for cooking fires when they couldn't find wood. (Buffalo chips)

❀ Samuel Clemens, Eugene Fields and George Washington Carver are some of its most famous sons. (Missouri)

♣ It's sometimes called "Old Man River." (Mississippi River)

★ The capital of New Mexico (Santa Fe)

♦ The busiest airport in America (O'Hare International in Chicago, Illinois)

❀ *He was the first left-handed President. (James Garfield)

♣ Name three of the four states that border Mexico. (New Mexico, Texas, California and Arizona)

★ Stephen Foster, who wrote over 200 plantation melodies, called this state his home. (Kentucky)

♦ America's number one "wheat" state (Kansas)

❀ This state grows more food than any other. (California)

♣ Most of the major league baseball teams conduct their spring training camps in this state. (Florida)

★ Canada lies to the north; Wyoming and Idaho lie to the south. (Montana)

♦ In which city is the Mayo Clinic located? (Rochester, Minnesota)

❀ The world's longest bridge crosses what lake in the United States? (Lake Pontchartrain in southern Louisiana)

♣ What sporting event begins with the command "Gentlemen, start your engines!"? (Indianapolis 500)

★ He wrote our national anthem. (Francis Scott Key)

♦ The name of America's first space shuttle (*Columbia*)

❀ The huge reservoir behind Hoover Dam (Lake Mead)

♣ In which state can one visit Old Faithful? (Wyoming)

★ Before it became a state in 1820, Maine was a part of this state. (Massachusetts)

♦ Waikiki Beach and Akaka Falls are located here. (Hawaii)

❀ The largest land area ever bought by the United States government (Louisiana Territory)

♣ America's number one country and western music city (Nashville, Tennessee)

★ Lake Champlain is located in the northwest corner of this state. (Vermont)

♦ The United States ranks fourth in land area. Name the three countries that are larger. (Soviet Union, China and Canada)

❀ Which city is the Chocolate Capital of America? (Hershey, Pennsylvania)

GA1157

48

GA1157

- ♣ The "City of Brotherly Love" (Philadelphia, Pennsylvania)

- ✪ *She wrote "America the Beautiful." (Katherine Lee Bates)

- ◆ The city of Indianola, located in this midwestern state, hosts the National Hot Air Balloon Championship. (Iowa)

- ❀ The world's first atomic bomb was tested in this state. (New Mexico)

- ♣ Which one of our states grows coffee? (Hawaii)

- ✪ Saginaw, Flint, Grand Rapids and Dearborn are cities here. (Michigan)

- ◆ This state leads the nation in potatoes. (Idaho)

- ❀ In which city is the U.S. Naval Academy located? (Annapolis, Maryland)

- ❀ The names of the three ships used on Columbus' first trip to the New World (*Nina, Pinta* and *Santa Maria*)

- ✪ He invented the cotton gin. (Eli Whitney)

- ◆ This river separates Ohio from Kentucky. (Ohio)

- ❀ The longest suspension bridge in the United States (Verrazano-Narrows Bridge in New York)

- ❀ Name the river that runs through the city of Washington, D.C. (Potomac)

- ✪ During his administration as President, the United States added California, New Mexico, Texas and the Oregon Territory. (James Polk)

- ◆ The "Little Town on the Prairie" (De Smet, South Dakota)

- ❀ *He started the twenty-one missions between San Diego and San Francisco. (Father Junipero Serra)

- ♣ The historical period following the Civil War between 1865-1877 (Reconstruction)

- ✪ Who said, "Old soldiers never die; they just fade away"? (General Douglas MacArthur)

- ◆ The Pine Tree State (Maine)

- ❀ The only state capital named after a saint (Saint Paul, Minnesota)

- ♣ He was called the "Captain of Industry" because of his domination of the oil refining business in the late 1800's. (John D. Rockefeller)

- ✪ What was the religion of William Penn? (Quaker of Religious Society of Friends)

- ◆ He established Maryland as a colony where freedom of religion was practiced. (Lord Baltimore)

- ❀ This President started the Peace Corps. (John F. Kennedy)

- ♣ The famous tavern in Williamsburg where George Washington and members of the Virginia House of Burgesses met (Raleigh Tavern)

- ✪ Who wrote the Pledge of Allegiance? (Francis Bellamy)

- ◆ What important day is observed traditionally on the third Sunday in June? (Father's Day)

- ❀ The first permanent settlement on the Gulf Coast (Biloxi, Mississippi)

- ♣ In which state do we find the source of the Mississippi River? (Minnesota)

- ✪ Name two of the three leaders of the Confederate States of America carved on Stone Mountain in Georgia. (Robert E. Lee, "Stonewall" Jackson and Jefferson Davis)

- ◆ The two prominent political figures assassinated in 1968 (Robert F. Kennedy and Dr. Martin Luther King, Jr.)

- ❀ Kentucky and Virginia lie to the north and Mississippi, Alabama and Georgia to the south. (Tennessee)

GA1157

50

- The most decorated hero of World War I (Sergeant Alvin York)

- The President who refused to allow American athletes to participate in the 1980 Moscow Olympics (Jimmy Carter)

- The mountains in South Dakota and Wyoming where gold was discovered in 1874 (Black Hills)

- This state's first territorial governor, William Henry Harrison, later became President, and then his grandson Benjamin Harrison also became President. (Indiana)

- The theater in which President Lincoln was shot (Ford's Theater)

- To which war was the cry "Remember the Maine" associated? (World War I)

- What was the fate of John Brown for his participation in the attack on Harpers Ferry? (He was hanged.)

- Land of the Midnight Sun, Seward's Folly and Walrussia all make reference to the same state. (Alaska)

- What do the letters *EPA* represent? (Environmental Protection Agency)

- The only President who was shot but survived an assassin's bullet (Ronald Reagan)

- The awards given by the Academy of Motion Picture Arts and Sciences (Academy Awards or Oscars)

- Will Rogers, Jim Thorpe and Johnny Tiger are some of its favorite sons. (Oklahoma)

- Professional baseball player forced to give up his career at the age of 35 because of illness after playing in a record 2130 consecutive games (Lou Gehrig)

- This city is sometimes referred to as the "Cradle of Jazz." (New Orleans, Louisiana)

- Jackson Square, Preservation Hall, the French Market and the Garden District are all a part of this fun-loving city. (New Orleans, Louisiana)

- The most widely known group of Mennonites (Amish)

- *He was the King of England when the colonies delcared their independence. (King George III)

- She was the first black Miss America. (Vanessa Williams)

- What is the process called that can remove a President from office? (Impeachment-Conviction)

- To the north lies Montana, to the south Utah and Colorado. (Wyoming)

- This state was the scene of the infamous Teapot Dome scandal in the 1920's. (Wyoming)

- The well-publicized Wall Drug is located in this state. (South Dakota)

- In which state is the Sun Valley ski resort located? (Idaho)

- Fort Sumter, where the Civil War began, is here, and this state was the first to secede. (South Carolina)

- In which U.S. city would one find Churchill Downs? (Louisville, Kentucky)

- In which state can one travel across Trail Ridge Road? (Colorado)

- This city has the largest Chinatown in the United States. (San Francisco, California)

- Which U.S. city played host to the 23rd Olympiad? (Los Angeles, California)

- How many guns are fired in a salute to the U.S. President? (21)

- The only man to have served as both Chief Justice of the U.S. Supreme Court and President of the United States (William Howard Taft)

- Name two of the three Presidents that were referred to by their initials. (Franklin D. Roosevelt, FDR; John F. Kennedy, JFK and Lyndon B. Johnson, LBJ)

- Mark Twain, the pen name of Samuel Clemen's, is "river talk" for a water depth of two fathoms. How deep would the water be? (12 feet; there are 6 feet in a fathom.)

52

♣ He led the American delegation to Paris to sign the peace treaty following the Revolution. (Benjamin Franklin)

✪ *This poet called the first shot of the Revolution "the shot heard round the world." (Ralph Waldo Emerson)

♦ The Evergreen State (Washington)

❀ What is the nickname used to refer to those who belong to the U.S. Marine Corps? (Leathernecks)

♣ The first black pitcher in major league baseball (Satchel Paige)

✪ Which war cost the United States the most money? (World War II)

♦ This state leads the nation in the production of salt. (Louisiana)

❀ The Wright Brothers made their first "successful" flight at Kitty Hawk in this state. (North Carolina)

♣ The only President elected unanimously by the Electoral College (George Washington)

✪ To which mountain system do the Cumberland Mountains belong? (Appalachians)

♦ What stadium do the Washington Redskins call home? (Robert F. Kennedy or RFK Stadium)

❀ Independence National Historic Park, the nation's most historic square mile, is located here. (Pennsylvania)

♣ Which U.S. city annually plays host to the Sugar Bowl? (New Orleans, Louisiana)

✪ Under the Land Ordinance of 1785, how many acres of land is a quarter section? (160 acres)

♦ He received the highest number of electoral votes ever in the Electoral College. (Ronald Reagan, 525 votes in 1984 presidential race)

❀ The capital of Colorado (Denver)

♣ Which state is named after a foreign country? (New Mexico)

✪ A scenic vacation choice in this state is The Dells. (Wisconsin)

♦ The historic significance of December 7, 1941 (The date Pearl Harbor was attacked by the Japanese)

❀ Custer took his last stand near the Little Bighorn River in this state. (Montana)

♣ In which U.S. city is the Super Dome located? (New Orleans, Louisiana)

✪ *The first U.S. President born west of the Mississippi (Herbert Hoover)

♦ Peachtree Street runs through the heart of the downtown area of this city. (Atlanta, Georgia)

❀ The Desert Inn, Stardust, The Golden Horseshoe and Caesar's Palace are here. (Las Vegas, Nevada)

♣ This agency of the U.S. government maintains the lighthouses and boats that patrol the U.S. coast. (U.S. Coast Guard)

✪ What product is Napa Valley in California best noted for? (Wine)

♦ After serving as governor of Alabama, he launched a campaign to win the presidency and an attempt was made on his life. (George Wallace)

❀ How many states are required to ratify an amendment to the Constitution? (¾ × 50 = 38)

♣ The famous route used by wagon trains between Independence, Missouri, and the Pacific Northwest (Oregon Trail)

✪ The Green Mountain State (Vermont)

♦ The mountains located between the Arkansas and Missouri Rivers (Ozark Mountains)

❀ The code name for the Allied Invasion of Normandy on D-Day (Operation Overland)

53

GA1157

54

GA1157

♣ Mount Rainier National Park is located in this state. (Washington)

★ Name two of the three axis powers of World War II. (Germany, Japan and Italy)

♦ The largest Amana settlement west of the Mississippi is located in this state. (Iowa)

❀ The last name of the two Presidents who were grandfather and grandson (Harrison)

♣ Carnegie Hall is located in this U.S. city. (New York City)

★ The site of the annual Hula Bowl (Honolulu, Hawaii)

♦ The state capital of Michigan (Lansing)

❀ In what year did San Francisco experience a devastating earthquake that killed over 700 people? (1906)

♣ The "Motion Picture Capital of the World" (Hollywood, California)

★ What do the letters NFL represent? (National Football League)

♦ Which state's name comes from the Cherokee Indian word for "meadowland"? (Kentucky)

❀ Name four of the seven Presidents born in Ohio. (McKinley, Harding, Benjamin Harrison, Garfield, Grant, Hayes and Taft)

♣ What is the nickname of the National League baseball team located in Canada? (Montreal Expos)

★ He has the distinction of being the only man to have been father to three U.S. senators. (Joseph Kennedy, Sr.)

♦ Who counts the votes of the Electoral College? (Vice president)

❀ Its western boundary includes Iowa and Missouri; its eastern boundary touches Indiana and Kentucky. (Illinois)

♣ What two foreign countries have left their influence on the city of New Orleans? (France and Spain)

★ The colony founded in 1733 by James Oglethorpe and named in honor of King George II (Georgia)

♦ He was commander of the Allied Forces in the southwest Pacific during World War II. (Douglas MacArthur)

❀ What is the official title of the person who serves as president of the U.S. Senate when the vice president is unable to attend? (President pro tempore)

♣ Which state flag has a single star that represents the time when it was a separate nation? (Texas)

★ What is the 200th anniversary of an event called? (Bicentennial)

♦ Name the club for boys that has as its motto "Be prepared." (Boy Scouts of America)

❀ The only man to be both President and vice president without going through an inauguration (Gerald Ford)

♣ The collective name of the first ten amendments to the U.S. Constitution (Bill of Rights)

★ *Which two Presidents are buried in Arlington National Cemetery? (William Howard Taft and John F. Kennedy)

♦ He wrote the classic Moby Dick. (Herman Melville)

❀ What nickname was used in reference to the confederate soldiers during the Civil War? (Rebels or Johnny Rebs)

♣ He invented the lightning rod. (Benjamin Franklin)

♦ Name the American Pima Indian who was one of the six men who raised the American flag on Mt. Suribachi. (Ira Hayes)

❀ This state leads the nation in tree farming. (Mississippi)

♣ The first U.S. President to ride to his inauguration in a car (Warren G. Harding)

GA1157

56

GA1157

♣ Where was the first modern-day Olympics held in 1896? (Athens, Greece)

✪ *He was nicknamed the "Swamp Fox" because he eluded the British by hiding in the marshes of South Carolina. (Francis Marion)

◆ In which state is Theodore Roosevelt National Park? (North Dakota)

❀ The Empire State Building, Rockefeller Center, the United Nations Building and the Metropolitan Opera are found in this city. (New York City)

♣ The tall trees in California (Redwoods)

✪ In this state is found the largest concrete dam, the Grand Coulee Dam. (Washington)

◆ This body of water separates Alaska from Russia. (Bering Strait)

❀ The capital city of Oregon (Salem)

♣ This state ranks number one in the production of toothpicks. (Maine)

✪ This state makes the most cigarettes. (North Carolina)

◆ The oldest college in the United States, it was founded in 1636. (Harvard)

❀ The first international hole-in-one was scored by George Wegener in 1934 when he teed off on the ninth hole in Canada and the ball found the cup in this state. (North Dakota)

♣ The "Red River Valley" is here. (North Dakota)

✪ This state boasts the only diamond mine in North America. (Arkansas)

◆ The Adirondack Mountains are here. (New York)

❀ The capital city of New Jersey (Trenton)

♣ The largest fresh water lake in North America (Lake Superior)

✪ New York is to the west and the Atlantic Ocean lies to the east (Massachusetts)

◆ This state was named by its first explorer, Ponce de Léon. (Florida)

❀ He wrote *Common Sense* calling for the colonies to declare their independence from England. (Thomas Paine)

♣ In which state is the Petrified Forest? (Arizona)

✪ The Townshend Acts were repealed by Parliament with the exception of the tax on this single commodity. (Tea)

◆ This state has beaches on both its east and west coasts. (Florida)

❀ This state has over twenty hours of sunshine during the summer months. (Alaska)

♣ Name four of the five states that form the American coastline on the Gulf of Mexico. (Texas, Alabama, Louisiana, Florida and Mississippi)

✪ The only President to have his inauguration ceremony at the White House (Franklin D. Roosevelt on his fourth inauguration)

◆ The last of the contiguous states to join the Union (Arizona)

❀ Craters of the Moon National Monument is located here. (Idaho)

♣ Name any of the three states that joined the Union during the Civil War. (Kansas, West Virginia and Nevada)

✪ The first state to join the Union after the original thirteen (Vermont in 1790)

◆ Arkansas and Missouri are on the west; North Carolina on the east. (Tennessee)

❀ This state ranks number one in people per square mile. (New Jersey)

GA1157

58

GA1157

♣ The number of senators in the United States Senate (100)

♣ Name the state on which your marker currently rests. (Verification by opposing player)

★ Kokomo, Gary and Terre Haute are all cities here. (Indiana)

★ This lake in Minnesota is the source of the mighty Mississippi. (Lake Itasca)

◆ The site in California where gold was first discovered (Sutter's Mill)

◆ This state has more land owned by the federal government than any other. (Alaska)

✿ This famous compromise during the Constitutional Convention brought about our bicameral system of making laws. (Connecticut Compromise)

✿ Its state university team's nickname is the Jayhawks. (Kansas)

♣ Our driest state (Nevada)

♣ In which state is Everglades National Park? (Florida)

★ What do the letters *SEATO* represent? (Southeast Asia Treaty Organization)

★ He sculpted the statue of Abraham Lincoln seated in a chair in the Lincoln Memorial. (Daniel Chester French)

◆ Lake Superior and Michigan lie to the north; Illinois to the south. (Wisconsin)

◆ An early attempt to settle this land by English colonists became known historically as the Lost Colony. (North Carolina)

✿ In which state is Denali National Park? (Alaska)

✿ He was "relieved" of his command during the Korean War by Harry S. Truman. (Douglas MacArthur)

♣ Name either of the two Presidents who were Quakers. (Herbert Hoover and Richard Nixon)

♣ Who fills the vacancy when one occurs in the office of vice president? (The President nominates a replacement subject to the approval of Congress.)

★ Name the city where the Preakness is run each year. (Pimlico, Maryland)

★ What building in Washington, D.C., serves as the reference point upon which all addresses in that city are based? (Capitol)

◆ This river flows from Pittsburgh, Pennsylvania, west into the Mississippi. (Ohio)

✿ The Monongahela National Forest is found in this state. (West Virginia)

✿ It was the first state to allow women the right to vote. (Wyoming)

✿ This state leads the nation in the number of counties. (Texas)

♣ The name of the airport in New York City once called Idlewild (John F. Kennedy International Airport)

♣ New York lies to the west; Rhode Island to the east. (Connecticut)

★ Which of these states would probably be of least concern to a presidential candidate—Kentucky, Ohio, California, Florida? (Kentucky)

★ If the correct time is 9:42 a.m. in New York City, what is the time in Seattle, Washington? (6:42 a.m.)

◆ The former home in Memphis, Tennessee, where rock and roll star Elvis Presley lived (Graceland)

◆ Which of the Ivy League schools is located in New Haven, Connecticut? (Yale University)

✿ The "City of Angels" (Los Angeles, California)

✿ The largest of our national parks, Wrangell-St. Elias, is located in this state. (Alaska)

59

GA1157

60

GA1157

♣ Which city is often called "Big D"? (Dallas, Texas)

★ The Flickertail State (North Dakota)

◆ To what organization do the letters *CIO* refer? (Congress of Industrial Organization)

❀ He was Ronald Reagan's vice president before becoming President himself. (George Bush)

♣ Those who visit North Cascades National Park are traveling in which state? (Washington)

★ The Kit Carson House, Taos Art Colony and Carlsbad Caverns are here. (New Mexico)

◆ The Twin Cities (Minneapolis and St. Paul, Minnesota)

❀ He was the main speaker at the dedication of the cemetery at Gettysburg, and he spoke for two hours. (Edward Everett)

♣ Cape Code National Seashore is located in this state. (Massachusetts)

★ The constitutional amendment that brought about Prohibition (Eighteenth)

◆ Name six of the thirteen original colonies. (New Hampshire, Connecticut, Delaware, New Jersey, New York, Massachusetts, Rhode Island, North Carolina, South Carolina, Georgia, Pennsylvania, Maryland and Virginia)

❀ The Mardi Gras is held here. (New Orleans, Louisiana)

♣ The only President sworn into office by a woman (Lyndon B. Johnson)

★ The mineral that made John D. Rockefeller, Sr., rich (Oil)

◆ This city is famous for its Cajun and Creole food. (New Orleans, Louisiana)

❀ This famous portrait painter painted the first five Presidents. (Gilbert Stuart)

♣ This peacekeeping organization was the forerunner of the United Nations. (League of Nations)

★ America's largest corporation (Exxon)

◆ Portsmouth is this state's only seaport. (New Hampshire)

❀ *William McKinley was assassinated in this city. (Buffalo, New York)

♣ He was the Emperor of France when the U.S. bought Louisiana. (Napoleon)

★ This term made reference to farmland on the Great Plains that was severely damaged by drought and dust storms during the 1930's. (Dust bowl)

◆ The Piscataqua, Merrimack and Sugar Rivers flow through this lovely New England state. (New Hampshire)

❀ *He was nicknamed "The Pathfinder." (John Charles Fremont)

♣ This Texas city is well-known for its "River Walk." (San Antonio, Texas)

★ In 1981 she became the first female justice to sit on the Supreme Court. (Sandra Day O'Connor)

◆ America's most famous zoo is located here. (San Diego, California)

❀ The state capital of Illinois (Springfield)

♣ This author received a Pulitzer prize for the only novel she ever wrote, *Gone with the Wind*. (Margaret Mitchell)

★ Great Smoky Mountains National Park is located in these two states. (North Carolina and Tennessee)

◆ Kentucky and Illinois are divided by this river. (Ohio)

❀ Eastport, Bangor, Lewiston and Brunswick are located here. (Maine)

GA1157

- ♣ The city where Martin Luther King, Jr., was assassinated (Memphis, Tennessee)

- ✪ She was the first woman to attempt to fly around the world. (Amelia Earhart)

- ♦ The National Football League franchise located in Seattle, Washington, uses what nickname for its team and logo? (Seahawks)

- ❀ To the north is Pennsylvania; to the south lies Virginia. (Maryland)

- ♣ Name the time zones that cover the contiguous United States. (Eastern, Central, Mountain and Pacific)

- ✪ It was the world's largest ship and it sank on its maiden voyage from England to the United States, killing over 1500 people because there weren't enough lifeboats. (*Titanic*)

- ♦ He was the first vice president to become President because of the death of the President. (John Tyler)

- ❀ The Magnolia State (Mississippi)

- ♣ The "Wizard of Menlo Park" (Thomas Edison)

- ✪ The nation's number one crude oil-producing state (Texas)

- ♦ The state where the acronym RAGBRAI has significance (Iowa)

- ❀ The mountain range that includes Yosemite National Park (Sierra Nevada Mountains)

- ♣ How many members are there on the U.S. Supreme Court? (9)

- ✪ Income Tax Day—the date when all federal income tax returns are due. (April 15)

- ♦ The city rocked by the earthquake of 1989 (San Francisco, California)

- ❀ This city is often called the "Motor City" because it is the automobile capital of the U.S. (Detroit, Michigan)

- ♣ The 1988 Winter Olympic Games were staged in this Canadian city. (Calgary)

- ✪ The official national flower of the United States (rose)

- ♦ Akron, Dayton, Springfield and Youngstown are located here. (Ohio)

- ❀ The fort in Baltimore Harbor over which the American flag was flying when Francis Scott Key wrote his famous poem (Fort McHenry)

- ♣ After Alaska, this state has the most miles of coastline. (Florida)

- ✪ The stadium the New York Mets call home (Shea Stadium)

- ♦ Custer National Forest, Yellowstone and Glacier National Parks are located here. (Montana)

- ❀ *He was called the "Ace of Aces" for his record of shooting down more enemy aircraft than anyone else during World War I. (Eddie Rickenbacker)

- ♣ To the south lie New Mexico and Oklahoma; to the north are Nebraska and Wyoming. (Colorado)

- ✪ The United States bought Florida from this European nation in 1819. (Spain)

- ♦ Oregon and Idaho lie to the north, California and Arizona to the south. (Nevada)

- ❀ America's tallest water fall (Yosemite Falls)

- ♣ What is the title of the presiding judge on the U.S. Supreme Court? (Chief Justice)

- ✪ The meaning of *E Pluribus Unum* which is found on U.S. coins (One out of many)

- ♦ The direction from which the trade winds come to the Hawaiian Islands (Northeast)

- ❀ This President is pictured on the nickel. (Thomas Jefferson)

GA1157

GA1157

- The state in which the Catskill Mountains are located (New York)

- The home state of Ethan Allen, early hero of American Revolution (Vermont)

- He was called the "Father of American Public Education" for his hard work and innovative ideas in education. (Horace Mann)

- The only President-elect to have an assassination attempt against his life before he was inaugurated. (Franklin D. Roosevelt)

- This state's song comes from a Broadway musical of the same name as the state. (Oklahoma)

- The symbol used by the U.S. Forest Service in its promotional materials to prevent forest fires (Smokey the Bear)

- What's Tuesday, October 29, 1929, more commonly called? (Black Tuesday)

- The Beehive State (Utah)

- In which city is Greenwich Village, an area well-known for its attraction for artists, writers, musicians and other friends of the arts? (New York City)

- Courthouse Rock and Chimney Rock are landmarks along the Oregon Trail found in this Great Plains state. (Nebraska)

- The Chattahoochee River serves as part of the boundary between these two states. (Georgia and Alabama)

- He was the first black man to win an Academy Award for his role in *Lilies of the Field*. (Sidney Poitier)

- President Kennedy was assassianted in this city. (Dallas, Texas)

- Illinois is on the west, and Ohio is to the east of this midwestern state. (Indiana)

- Name the three major mountain ranges west of the Mississippi. (Rocky Mountains, Sierra Nevada Mountains and Cascade Range)

- This river forms much of the boundary between Oregon and Washington. (Columbia)

- Famous vacation island located twenty-six miles off the coast of Los Angeles (Catalina Island)

- This department store in New York City claims to be the "largest in the United States." (Macy's)

- What does the department of our government referred to by the letters *HUD* stand for? (Housing and Urban Development)

- Although he was defeated for the presidency by John F. Kennedy, he later became President. (Richard Nixon)

- The unstable "fault" that lies beneath California causing most of the earthquakes between San Francisco south to Mexico (San Andreas Fault)

- Lake Superior and the Menominee River are on the north, while the Mississippi and St. Croix Rivers are on the west. (Wisconsin)

- The only President to be married in the White House (Grover Cleveland)

- Between which two of our Great Lakes is Niagara Falls located? (Lake Erie and Lake Ontario)

- The unofficial title of the President's wife? (First Lady)

- What is the dividing line between the northern and southern hemispheres? (Equator)

- What is the official motto of the United States? (In God We Trust)

- Ketchikan, Kodiak, Valdez and Sitka are located here. (Alaska)

- What U.S. city other than Los Angeles has played host to the Summer Olympic Games? (St. Louis, Missouri)

- King's Island amusement park boasts of "The Beast," the world's longest roller coaster. Near what city is this amusement park located? (Cincinnati, Ohio)

- These two men explored the Louisiana Territory shortly after it was bought from Napoleon. (Meriwether Lewis and William Clark)

- Chicago's downtown area bordered by an elevated train ("The Loop")

GA1157

66

♣ "Anchors Aweigh" is the official song of which branch of the military service? (U.S. Navy)

✪ To the north lies South Dakota; to the south are Colorado and Kansas. (Nebraska)

◆ How many red stripes and how many white stripes are on the American flag? (Seven red stripes and six white stripes)

❀ This former President has the distinction of having the most children, 15. (John Tyler)

♣ *He was a U.S. senator *after* he was President. (Andrew Johnson)

✪ Which U.S. national park joins Waterton Lakes National Park (in Canada) at the border in Montana? (Glacier National Park)

◆ The capital city of Kansas (Topeka)

❀ Near which city does the Missouri River empty into the Mississippi? (St. Louis, Missouri)

❀ How often does the U.S. government take a census? (Every ten years)

✪ *This President always wore a red carnation and a white vest when he made appearances in public. (William McKinley)

◆ The peninsula that extends out beyond the mainland of Massachusetts into Nantucket Sound (Cape Cod)

❀ The Columbia, Snake and Yakima Rivers flow through this state. (Washington)

❀ Which country did the United States fight in the War of 1812? (England)

✪ The Strasburg Railroad, Roadside America and Valley Forge are tourist attractions in this state. (Pennsylvania)

◆ If a military time is posted at "1500 hours," what is the corresponding civilian time? (3:00 p.m.)

❀ Famous railroad engineer who died trying to save the Cannonball Express (John Luther Jones better known as "Casey" Jones)

♣ America's "Insurance City" (Hartford, Connecticut)

✪ When a former President dies, how many days is the flag flown at half-mast? (30 days)

◆ What do the letters *FDIC* stand for? (Federal Deposit Insurance Corporation)

❀ More Presidents are alumni of this university than any other. (Harvard)

♣ Former President nicknamed "Silent Cal" (Calvin Coolidge)

✪ Name the state capital that is farther north than any other. (Juneau, Alaska)

◆ Name the state capital that is farther south than any other. (Honolulu, Hawaii)

❀ Dinosaur and Hovenweep National Monuments are found in these states. (Colorado and Utah)

♣ Name the state capital that is farther west than any other. (Honolulu, Hawaii)

✪ Name the state capital that is farther east than any other. (Augusta, Maine)

◆ The first permanent English settlement in the colonies (Jamestown, Virginia)

❀ The world's largest model railroad collection is located in this Tennessee city. (Chattanooga, Tennessee)

♣ The world's largest balloon rally is held each year in this state's largest city. (Santa Fe, New Mexico)

✪ This state ranks number one in rainfall with over 460 inches annually. (Hawaii)

◆ In 1979 the U.S. mint began stamping out $1 coins with the portrait of the only woman ever placed on a coin. What was her name? (Susan B. Anthony)

❀ The black athlete who won four gold medals at the 1936 Olympic Games. (Jesse Owens)

68

GA1157

♣ Seton Hall, Rutgers and the four "Oranges" are located in this state. (New Jersey))

✪ Near Mount Rushmore stands the beginning of a memorial to this great Sioux Indian chief. The unfinished sculpture is the dream of Korczak Ziolkowski. (Chief Crazy Horse)

♦ This state's name has only one syllable. (Maine)

❀ Name three of the four state capitals named after former Presidents. (Lincoln, NE; Jefferson City, MO; Madison, WI and Jackson, MS)

❀ The German zeppelin that crashed and burned in the United States in 1937 (*Hindenburg*)

✪ The capital city of Kentucky (Frankfort)

♦ His parents named him Hiram Ulysses, but he changed his name to Ulysses Simpson before he became President. (Ulysses S. Grant)

❀ In which city could one visit Nob Hill? (San Francisco, California)

☘ How many rings are in the symbol of the Olympic Games? (5)

✪ The *Mayflower* landed here in 1620. (Plymouth, Massachusetts)

♦ Martha's Vineyard and Nantucket Island are part of this state. (Massachusetts)

❀ He became the first (and only) American to become a world chess champion in 1972. (Bobby Fischer)

☘ This river forms the western boundary of Illinois. (Mississippi)

✪ The President well-known for his "fireside chats" which he presented to the nation on the radio (Franklin D. Roosevelt)

♦ Famous sea captain who said, "I have not yet begun to fight" (John Paul Jones)

❀ You can visit Grand Teton National Park in this state. (Wyoming)

♣ Hannibal Hamlin was once governor of this state. He later became vice president. (Maine)

✪ The name of the President's airplane (*Air Force One*)

♦ The Transcontinental Railroad was completed here in 1869. (Promontory, Utah)

❀ *Name the historical incident in which Crispus Attucks was killed. (Boston Massacre)

☘ She wrote the controversial *Uncle Tom's Cabin*, said by many to have been a cause of the Civil War. (Harriet Beecher Stowe)

✪ He wrote "The Star-Spangled Banner" while he watched the Americans repel the British near Baltimore. (Francis Scott Key)

♦ Guadalupe Mountains National Park is located in this state. (Texas)

❀ He was the sculptor of Mount Rushmore. (Gutzon Borglum)

☘ The European country to first raise its flag over Mississippi (Spain)

✪ By constitutional decree, he presides over the U.S. Senate. (Vice president)

♦ Name the plane built by financial mogul Howard Hughes acclaimed the largest plane ever built. (*Spruce Goose*)

❀ The relationship of Theodore and Franklin D. Roosevelt (Fifth cousins. Accept cousins.)

☘ The lowest geographical location in the United States (Death Valley)

✪ The largest state east of the Mississippi River (Georgia)

♦ The home state of both John Wayne and Johnny Carson (Iowa)

❀ *The organization formed in 1772 to keep the colonies informed of Great Britain's actions to enforce tax laws (Committees of Correspondence)

GA1157

70

♣ The Soo Canal separates this state from Canada. (Michigan)

✪ The Dutchman who bought Manhattan Island from the Indians for approximately $24 in goods (Peter Minuit)

♦ He ran for reelection to the presidency on the campaign slogan "He kept us out of war." (Woodrow Wilson)

❀ The city where Macy's Thanksgiving Day Parade takes place each year on Thanksgiving Day (New York City)

♣ The city to which one would travel to visit the Liberty Bell (Philadelphia, Pennsylvania)

✪ The term used to describe a state which nominates a candidate from its own state at the national party convention (Favorite son)

♦ What's the meaning of the acronym *MARTA*? (Metropolitan Atlantic Rapid Transit Authority)

❀ The home state of George Custer, Clarence Darrow and Johnny Appleseed (Ohio)

♣ The historic flight of the Wright Brothers took place near this North Carolina city. (Kitty Hawk)

✪ This state leads the nation in the production of lumber. (Oregon)

♦ Three of the five entrances to the nation's oldest national park (Yellowstone) are located here. (Montana)

❀ What was the nickname of President Lyndon B. Johnson's wife? ("Lady Bird")

❀ Steel magnate who built a famous concert hall in New York City bearing his name (Andrew Carnegie)

✪ The Buckeye State (Ohio)

♦ On July 4, 1946, who did the United States grant independence to? (The Philippines)

❀ America's gambling capital (Nevada. Accept Las Vegas.)

♣ *According to the flag code, what is the ratio of the length of the flag to the width? (1.9 to 1.0)

✪ His New Deal was engineered to end the Depression. (Franklin D. Roosevelt)

♦ The nationality of Christopher Columbus, the man who discovered the Americas (Italian)

❀ He was the only President ever to have been the head of a union. (Ronald Reagan)

♣ The Equality State (Wyoming)

✪ What was the name of the play Abraham Lincoln was viewing when he was assassinated? (*Our American Cousin*)

♦ Probably the first white man to explore what is now Vermont (Samuel de Champlain)

❀ In what state would you find the boyhood home of Henry Wadsworth Longfellow, the famous poet? (Maine)

♣ He is credited with the invention of the telephone. (Alexander Graham Bell)

✪ Golden Spike National Historic Site is found in this state. (Utah)

♦ The first European to see the Grand Canyon (Francisco Vásquez de Coronado)

❀ He was victorious at the Battle of New Orleans. (Andrew Jackson)

❀ *He assassinated President William McKinley on September 6, 1901. (Leon Czolgosz)

✪ The term used to describe the power of a President to reject a bill that has been approved by Congress (Veto)

♦ The state where Chimney Rock and Homestead National Monument are located (Nebraska)

❀ The first President to live in the White House (John Adams)

GA1157

72

GA1157

- ♣ The capital city of Arizona (Phoenix)

- ✪ The bird that symbolizes peace (Dove)

- ♦ His name was William F. Cody. He was better remembered by his nickname. (Buffalo Bill)

- ✿ Describe the configuration of stars on the American flag. (Five rows of six stars and four rows of five stars)

- ♣ This U.S. city is often referred to as the "financial capital of the world." (New York City)

- ✪ Both the Grand Canyon and Petrified Forest National Parks are located here. (Arizona)

- ♦ Name either of the two former Presidents who lived to the age of 90. (John Adams and Herbert Hoover)

- ✿ To what date was FDR referring when he described it as ". . . a date which will live in infamy"? (December 7, 1941—the attack on Pearl Harbor by Japan)

- ♣ From which document do these words come "We the people of the United States. . . ." (U.S. Constitution)

- ✪ When he became President there were forty-eight stars on the flag; when he left the presidency, there were fifty. (Dwight D. Eisenhower)

- ♦ Exaggerated reports of the discovery of gold caused Pikes Peak Gold Rush here. (Colorado)

- ✿ On whose grave does the eternal flame burn? (John F. Kennedy)

- ♣ He was the Secretary of State who engineered the deal to buy Alaska from Russia. (William H. Seward)

- ✪ Almost everyone is familiar with the name of Franklin D. Roosevelt. Name the other Franklin who became President. (Franklin Pierce)

- ♦ He was President when the United States declared war on Mexico. (James Polk)

- ✿ Garrison Dam, the Red River, Lake Sakakawea and the Battle of the Little Bighorn are all found here. (North Dakota)

- ♣ What was the most important crop grown on Jimmy Carter's farm? (Peanuts)

- ✪ He was the youngest President to die. (John F. Kennedy, 46)

- ♦ Name either of the Presidents elected from the Whig Party. (Zachary Taylor and William H. Harrison)

- ✿ Daniel Webster and Franklin Pierce were two of its favorite sons. (New Hampshire)

- ♣ This amendment to the U.S. Constitution guaranteed citizenship to former slaves. (Fourteenth)

- ✪ This President learned to read from his wife who was a school teacher. (Andrew Johnson)

- ♦ The home state of the world's tallest office building (Illinois, the Sears Tower in Chicago)

- ✿ From what country did the United States buy the land contained in the Gadsden Purchase? (Mexico)

- ♣ The team name of the Chicago franchise that is a part of the National Football League (Bears)

- ✪ What is the simple mathematical rule to remember when a presidential election will be held? (All years that can be divided evenly by four)

- ♦ The artist who painted most of the more famous paintings of George Washington (Gilbert Stuart)

- ✿ He founded Tuskegee Institute. (Booker T. Washington)

- ♣ The state bird of Maryland is also the name of its major league baseball team. (Baltimore Oriole)

- ✪ The most significant geologic occurrence on October 17, 1989 (The earthquake in San Francisco, California)

- ♦ In which state was Abraham Lincoln born? (Kentucky)

- ✿ The building where the Declaration of Independence and the Constitution are kept (National Archives)

GA1157

74

♣ This fun park near Los Angeles was little more than a good place to buy souvenir jams and jellies a few years ago. (Knott's Berry Farm)

✪ The capital of Mississippi (Jackson)

◆ The battleship on which the Japanese signed the surrender ending World War II (*USS Missouri*)

❀ She was called "Hanoi Jane." (Jane Fonda)

♣ This capital city has the name of the state contained in its name. (Indianapolis, Indiana)

✪ This state leads the nation in the production of steel. (Indiana)

◆ This river serves as the western boundary of Iowa. (Missouri)

❀ The city in Massachusetts founded by the Puritans that is historically remembered for its trials of witchcraft (Salem)

♣ *The tallest mountain east of the Mississippi (Mt. Mitchell in North Carolina)

✪ This city has a famous street called "The Strip." (Las Vegas, Nevada)

◆ The tallest mountains in the Appalachian Mountain System (Great Smoky Mountains)

❀ This state's name is the Algonquin word for *Great Lake*. (Michigan)

♣ Sandwiched between Pennsylvania and West Virginia to the east and Indiana to the west (Ohio)

✪ Identify the meaning of the acronym *SALT* (Strategic Arms Limitation Talks)

◆ Name either of the two men who became vice president without facing the test of an election. (Gerald Ford and Nelson Rockefeller)

❀ This First Lady did not have to change her name when she married. (Eleanor Roosevelt)

♣ Famous Texan who served a record seventeen years as Speaker of the House (Sam Rayburn)

✪ The Treaty of Guadalupe Hidalgo brought an end to this war. (War with Mexico)

◆ The state in which Glacier National Park is located (Montana)

❀ The valley north of San Francisco known for its high quality of wines (Napa Valley)

♣ This state lists Badlands National Park as one of its tourist attractions. (South Dakota)

✪ The annual speech the President delivers to Congress each January (State of the Union Address)

◆ One of its famous streets is named Bourbon Street. (New Orleans, Louisiana)

❀ The state capital of Nevada (Carson City)

♣ The largest of the Hawaiian Islands (Hawaii)

✪ Carlsbad Caverns National Park is one of the main tourist attractions of this state. (New Mexico)

◆ The site where the first battle of the Revolution was fought on April 19, 1775 (Lexington, Massachusetts)

❀ America's largest metropolitan area (New York City)

♣ The street in Chicago called "The Magnificent Mile" (Michigan Avenue)

✪ Most important mountains to Vermonters (Green Mountains)

◆ The campaign slogan of those who supported Dwight D. Eisenhower ("I like Ike")

❀ America's largest river gorge (Grand Canyon)

GA1157

76

♣ The Norwegian explorer who possibly discovered the continent of North America about 1000 A.D. (Leif Eriksson)

★ Oklahoma lies to the west, and Tennessee and Mississippi to the east. (Arkansas)

◆ *The first Black to graduate from the University of Mississippi, his college years became a focal point of the nation because of the federal troops stationed on campus to protect him. (James Meredith)

❋ Most of the laborers who worked on the Central Pacific Railroad section of the Transcontinental Railroad were from what country? (China)

❋ The headquarters of the Mormon Church are found in this state. (Utah)

★ Name three of the four states that start with the letter I. (Illinois, Indiana, Iowa and Idaho)

◆ The highest rank to which a Boy Scout can aspire (Eagle Scout)

❋ Following the assassination of James Garfield, the Civil Service Reform Bill was enacted with the help and support of this President. (Chester Arthur)

♣ He wrote "God Bless America." (Irving Berlin)

★ Name either of the two places in the United States where the Winter Olympic Games have been held. (Lake Placid, New York and Squaw Valley, California)

◆ The President who pushed hard for the purchase of the Louisiana Territory, because he thought it was too good a deal to turn down (Thomas Jefferson)

❋ The capital city of North Carolina (Raleigh)

♣ To what does the acronym *NATO* refer? (North Atlantic Treaty Organization)

★ Famous Union general who made a devastating "march to the sea" during the Civil War (General William T. Sherman)

◆ The "bachelor President" who never married (James Buchanan)

❋ Massachusetts lies to the north and Long Island is on the south. (Connecticut)

♣ St. Joseph, Springfield, Moberly and Joplin are all located here. (Missouri)

★ The President's group of advisors (Cabinet)

◆ The last man to become President without a college degree (Harry S. Truman)

❋ *He was the President nicknamed "Old Rough and Ready." (Zachary Taylor)

❋ The constitutional amendment that gave former slaves the right to vote (Fifteenth)

★ Alan Shepard, Horace Greeley and Salmon Chase all called this state home. (New Hampshire)

◆ Our tallest President, he stood 6 feet, 4 inches. (Abraham Lincoln)

❋ America's southernmost city (Hilo, Hawaii)

♣ Our heaviest President, weighing over 300 pounds (William Howard Taft)

★ The first man from the South to win the presidency since the Civil War (Jimmy Carter)

◆ Nickname for opportunist Northerners who went to the South following the Civil War to claim political positions and take advantage of economic chaos (Carpetbaggers)

❋ The oldest city in the United States (St. Augustine, Florida, founded in 1565)

♣ The President who graduated from the Naval Academy (Jimmy Carter)

★ *She was named the Outstanding Woman Athlete in the First Half of the 1900's for her achievements. (Babe Didrikson Zaharias)

◆ Alphabetically, the first state listed is Alabama. Which state is last on the list? (Wyoming)

❋ The second most visited park in the USA is in Maine. (Acadia)

78

♣ The state capital of Maryland (Annapolis)

★ He established the Dutch claim to America. (Henry Hudson)

◆ Name the five states that touch the Pacific Ocean. (Alaska, California, Hawaii, Oregon and Washington)

✿ The famous gunfighter who was killed playing poker, his last hand being two aces and two eights—known ever since as the "dead man's hand" (Wild Bill Hickok)

♣ From what European country did the United States buy the Virgin Islands? (Denmark)

★ Council Bluffs, Waterloo, Sioux City and Burlington are located here. (Iowa)

◆ This river ranks second behind the mighty Mississippi in length. (Missouri)

✿ Into what body of water does the Potomac River empty? (Chesapeake Bay)

✿ What name was used to describe those who were given free passage to America from Europe in exchange for their labor for a period of time up to seven years? (Indentured servants)

★ What word is used to describe a legislature composed of two houses? (Bicameral)

◆ This Great Lake separates the upper peninsula from the lower peninsula. (Lake Michigan)

✿ This state leads the nation in citrus fruits. (Florida)

✿ The charter that established the United Nations was drafted in this city. (San Francisco, California)

★ With representation in the House based on population, what is the least number of representatives a state may have? (1)

◆ In which state would one travel to visit Haleakala National Park? (Hawaii)

✿ Which of these issues would be the most sensitive to the voters of Iowa: illegal aliens, offshore oil rights, farm prices or water pollution? (Farm prices)

♣ In Dearborn, Michigan, the group of restored historical buildings significant to the automobile industry in early America (Greenfield Village)

★ The Big Sky Country (Montana)

◆ Name the two largest news-gathering wire services in the United States. (Associated Press [AP] and United Press International [UPI])

✿ In 1867 the farmers of America united to form an organization called the . . . . (Grange)

♣ The minimum number of electoral votes to which a state is entitled (3)

★ Under Executive Order 956 during World War II, anyone who was a descendant of this country was forced to live in a "relocation" camp. (Japan)

◆ This state shares Lake Tahoe with California. (Nevada)

✿ Yellow ribbons were tied "'round the old oak trees" and other trees as well as a symbol of welcome to what group of people coming home to America? (Hostages from Iran)

♣ Name three of the four former U.S. Presidents whose names are the most often used to name streets. (Washington, Lincoln, Jefferson and Madison)

★ The "City by the Bay" (San Francisco, California)

◆ Name the high speed testing ground for automobiles on the Great Salt Lake Desert in Utah. (Bonneville Salt Flats)

✿ The state capital of Hawaii (Honolulu)

♣ The only New England state without a coastline on the Atlantic (Vermont)

★ Name three of the four Presidents who have been assassinated. (Lincoln, Garfield, McKinley and Kennedy)

◆ Name one of the three most visited of our national parks. (Great Smoky Mountains, Yosemite and Acadia)

✿ Which amendment to the Constitution gave Congress the power to tax the income of Americans? (Sixteenth)

GA1157

♣ Because of his loathe for monopolies, this President earned the nickname "Trust Buster." (Theodore Roosevelt)

✪ In which state could one see the wildlife of Lake Okeechobee. (Florida)

♦ The capital city of Texas (Austin)

❀ He was the first black man to play major league baseball. (Jackie Robinson)

♣ *Her real name was Mary Ludwig Hays, but she was better known by another name that related to her carrying pitchers of water to soldiers during the Revolution. What was her nickname? (Molly Pitcher)

✪ Which constitutional amendment assures that there will always be a vice president? (Twenty-fifth)

♦ Most states have regional units of government called counties, but what does Louisiana call such units? (Parishes)

❀ Mark Twain, Charles Goodyear and Ethan Allen all had this state in common. (Massachusetts)

♣ On what religious holiday was Abraham Lincoln assassinated? (Good Friday)

✪ He was called the "Father of the American Textile Industry." (Samuel Slater)

♦ Name the railroad system that is sponsored in part by the federal government. (AMTRAK)

❀ America's first successful steamboat built by Robert Fulton (Clermont)

♣ America's largest bird of prey—it is nearly extinct. (California condor)

✪ What music is played during the awards ceremony when the medals are awarded after an event in the Olympics? (The national anthem of the country of the gold medal winner)

♦ Describe the significance of these ships: Susan Constant, Discovery and Godspeed. (They were the ships used by the settlers who came to Jamestown in 1607.)

❀ The Grand Ole Opry and theme park called Opryland are located in this city. (Nashville, Tennessee)

♣ In which state would one travel to visit Bryce Canyon National Park? (Utah)

✪ Where do the electors meet to cast their votes for President in the Electoral College? (They meet in their respective state capitals. The ballots are then sent to Washington, D.C., to be counted.)

♦ The world's longest tunnel-bridge system (Chesapeake Bay, Bridge-Tunnel)

❀ What was the home state of Jefferson Davis, president of the Confederacy? (Mississippi)

♣ To what historic military event did this signal refer? "One if by land, two if by sea"? (The warning from the Old North Church to Paul Revere of the approaching British during the Revolution)

✪ He said, "Ask not what your country can do for you— ask what you can do for your country." (John F. Kennedy)

♦ The expensive shellfish for which Maine is best noted (Lobster)

❀ W.I.N. buttons (Whip Inflation Now) were worn by the supporters of this President. (Gerald Ford)

♣ Name the American who served as chairman of the foundation that helped to raise millions of dollars to restore the Statue of Liberty and Ellis Island. (Lee Iacocca)

✪ The Old Line State (Maryland)

♦ Under the Land Ordinance of 1785, how many acres were in a half section of land? (320 acres)

❀ The cities of Grand Island, Ogallala and Scottsbluff are located here. (Nebraska)

♣ The state capital of Ohio (Columbus)

✪ The only President sworn into office while he was aboard an airplane (Lyndon B. Johnson)

♦ What is the minimum length of time a member of the House of Representatives must have been a U.S. citizen? (7 years)

❀ A list of the Presidents in alphabetical order would find this man heading the list. (John Adams)

82

♣ The state capital of Montana (Helena)

✪ This state's name is the plural of an Indian tribe that once lived here. It is the only state whose name is a plural word. (Massachusetts)

♦ What was the forced relocation of the Cherokee Indians from their homes east of the Mississippi to Oklahoma called? (The Trail of Tears)

❀ The English trading company that founded Jamestown (London Company)

❀ The name of Walt Disney's first sound cartoon ("Steamboat Willie")

✪ What is the most important source of revenue to Nevada? (Gambling)

♦ Name the state on which your marker now rests. (Verification by opposing player)

❀ What agency of the federal government is better known by the acronym *FHA*? (Federal Housing Administration)

♣ This state leads the nation in textile production. (North Carolina)

✪ What is the term used when the President simply retains a bill sent to him by Congress because it is within the last ten days of session? (Pocket veto)

♦ The Aloha State (Hawaii)

❀ He is the "winningest coach" in college football with 323 career wins. (Paul "Bear" Bryant)

♣ The annual football game between the champion of the National Football Conference (NFC) and American Football Conference (AFC) (Super Bowl)

✪ The length of the term of office for a United States senator (6 years)

♦ Iowa is on its northern border; Arkansas lies to the south. (Missouri)

❀ What state honors the fiddle as its state instrument? (Arkansas)

♣ Long Island and the Hudson Valley are located here. (New York)

✪ He probably explored the coastline of Maine in 1498. (John Cabot)

♦ The largest of America's domed stadiums (Super Dome in New Orleans, Louisiana)

❀ He was the first to sign the Declaration of Independence, and his name has been synonymous with signatures ever since. (John Hancock)

♣ The beverage choice of Americans (Soft drinks)

✪ This state leads the nation in the production of paper. (Georgia)

♦ The home state of Charlton Heston, Tom Selleck and Diana Ross (Michigan)

❀ These Japanese suicide pilots of World War II purposely flew their planes into American ships. (Kamikaze)

♣ *He was nicknamed "Old Fuss and Feathers," but in reality he was a powerful military leader. (Winfield Scott)

✪ This state usually hosts the first presidential primary. (New Hampshire)

♦ The most prestigious award that can be given to somone in the armed forces (Congressional Medal of Honor)

❀ *This state has often been called the "Mother of Presidents." (Ohio)

♣ To the east are Connecticut, Massachusetts and Vermont; to the West are a part of Pennsylvania and a part of Canada. (New York)

✪ Singer Ray Charles made Georgia's state song popular all over America with his recording. Name the song. ("Georgia on My Mind")

♦ The first state to secede from the United States before the Civil War began (South Carolina in December, 1860)

❀ To what do the letters *GNP* refer? (Gross National Product—The total value of all the goods and services produced by a country within a given time)

GA1157

♣ In which U.S. city was the World's Columbian Exposition held to honor the fortieth year of Columbus discovering the Americas? (Chicago, Illinois)

✪ *What was the name of the treaty that formally ended the War of 1812? (Treaty of Ghent)

◆ Quote the rule on the precise date when presidential elections are held. (On the Tuesday following the first Monday in November of all years evenly divisible by four)

✿ He coached the famed Notre Dame University football teams during the 1920's. (Knute Rockne)

♣ The swamp located in both Georgia and Florida (Okefenokee Swamp)

✪ A political division that places all the voters within the boundary voting in the same place (Precinct)

◆ The chain of islands off the southwest coast of Alaska (Aleutian Islands)

✿ He is known historically for betraying his country during the Revolution. (Benedict Arnold)

♣ The name of the French sculptor who deisgned the Statue of Liberty (Frederic Auguste Bartholdi. Accept last name.)

✪ What nationality was the genius Albert Einstein? (German)

◆ Name the scale that is used to measure the intensity of earthquakes. (Richter scale)

✿ *This famous painting by Grant Wood depicts a farmer holding a pitchfork standing next to his wife. (American Gothic)

♣ Where could one visit the French Quarter? (New Orleans, Louisiana)

✪ In what year will the next census be taken? (Under the Constitution, it is required that a census be conducted every ten years in the year that begins each decade. For example, 1990, 2000, etc.)

◆ This river serves as the boundary between Iowa and Nebraska. (Missouri)

✿ The boyhood hometown of Mark Twain (Hannibal, Missouri)

♣ This company builds most of the commercial aircraft that fly America's skies. (Boeing)

✪ On May 25, 1986, America formed a human chain across the country to raise money for the poor. What was the effort called? (Hands Across America)

◆ She was called "Lemonade Lucy" because she refused to allow alcohol in the White House and served lemonade instead. (Lucy Hayes)

✿ What agency is represented by the letters NASA? (National Aeronautics and Space Administration)

♣ The name of the comic strip created by Charles Schultz that captured the hearts of Americans during the 1970's and 80's. ("Peanuts")

✪ Name two of three states that begin with the letter O. (Oregon, Oklahoma and Ohio)

◆ What metal was used for the outside of the Statue of Liberty? (Copper)

✿ The plane in which Charles Lindbergh flew across the Atlantic (Spirit of St. Louis)

♣ Name America's three largest metropolitan areas in no particular order. (New York City, Los Angeles and Chicago)

✪ Under the Constitution which house of Congress conducts the trial when someone has been impeached? (U.S. Senate)

◆ Name the three horse races that constitute the Triple Crown. (Kentucky Derby, Preakness and Belmont Stakes)

✿ What time zone is represented by the letters PST? (Pacific Standard Time)

♣ She saved Captain John Smith from being killed by her father. (Pocahontas)

✪ He gave us the Fair Deal. (Harry S. Truman)

◆ This river separates Georgia from South Carolina. (Savannah)

✿ What does the color white represent on the American flag? (Accept purity or innocence.)

GA1157

♣ His name was John Chapman, but his planting of a certain kind of fruit tree across America earned him another name. (Johnny Appleseed)

✪ In what U.S. state is the London Bridge now located? (Arizona)

♦ This island separates the American Falls and the Canadian Falls at Niagara Falls and serves as part of the border between the two countries. (Goat Island)

❁ He was simply called "Boss" because of his power and influence over Chicago politics during his tenure as mayor. (Richard Daley)

♣ *As he retracted from the Philippines in 1942, he spoke these words which would someday be well remembered: "I shall return." (General Douglas MacArthur)

✪ Olympic National Park is located here. (Washington)

♦ This city in Texas serves as the training center for America's astronauts. (Houston, Texas)

❁ The most popular outdoor participation sport in America (Golf)

❁ Lake Champlain serves as part of the boundary between Vermont and what other state? (New York)

✪ To what issue did the famous 1954 Supreme Court decision in the case Brown vs. Board of Education of Topeka refer? (Racial segregation in schools was declared illegal.)

♦ He was the first President to be affected by the twenty-second amendment limiting a President to two terms in office. (Dwight D. Eisenhower)

❁ Carl Bernstein and Bob Woodward from the *Washington Post* became famous for what reason? (They uncovered the Watergate incident.)

❁ He was wounded in the same motorcade in which President Kennedy was assassinated. (John B. Connally)

✪ In which city would one be to attend a performance in Radio City Music Hall? (New York City)

♦ *He was President when the United States annexed the territory of Hawaii in 1900. (William McKinley)

❁ What is the "calm" in the center of a hurricane called? (The eye)

♣ The annual series of playoff games between the American and National League Baseball Champions (World Series)

✪ In which of our national parks is Old Faithful—America's most famous geyser? (Yellowstone)

♦ This famous eastern "vacation city" has a boardwalk along its beach. (Atlantic City, New Jersey)

❁ American Indian who was voted the Greatest Athlete of the First Half of the Century (Jim Thorpe)

♣ What word is used to describe those who explore caves? (Spelunkers)

✪ The most recent President of those who earned a spot on Mount Rushmore (Theodore Roosevelt)

♦ America's number one cheese state (Wisconsin)

❁ This state has an upper peninsula and a lower peninsula. (Michigan)

♣ Its location is on an island in San Francisco Bay, and in days past it was a federal prison. (Alcatraz)

✪ New York City street that is famous for its musicals and plays (Broadway)

♦ What is pictured on the opposite side of an Indian head nickel? (Buffalo)

❁ What do we call the President's office? (The Oval Office)

❁ In what city is the National Zoo? (Washington, D.C.)

✪ Mesa Verde National Park is located in which state? (Colorado)

♦ He is the only man elected two times to the vice presidency and later elected twice to the presidency. (Richard Nixon)

❁ John W. Hinkley attempted to assassinate him but failed. (Ronald Reagan)

GA1157

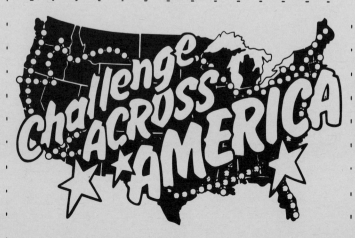

88

♣ He was both the shortest President and the President who weighed the least. (James Madison)

✪ Of those who signed the Constitution, he was the oldest and certainly one of the wisest. (Benjamin Franklin)

♦ Japan gave over 6000 of these trees to the United States for planting in the nation's capital, where they have become a springtime tradition. (Cherry trees)

❀ What is the word used to describe the only way the U.S. Constitution can be changed? (Amendment)

☘ *He was the first American to orbit the earth. (John Glenn, February 20, 1962)

✪ He introduced tobacco to the colonies as a crop in Virginia, and it soon became their financial salvation. (John Rolfe)

♦ Give the date which we annually designate as Flag Day. (June 14)

❀ The two generals who signed the terms of surrender that ended the Civil War at Appomattox Court House. (Robert E. Lee and Ulysses S. Grant)

❀ The number of electoral votes needed to win the presidency (270)

✪ A part of his program to stabilize the economy was "Win Gardens." (Gerald Ford)

♦ Name the two states in which Hoover Dam is located. (Nevada and Arizona)

❀ Most of the aircraft flown by America's major airlines are made by Boeing in this Washington city. (Seattle)

☘ He mistakenly called the Native Americans "Indians." (Christopher Columbus, who thought he had reached Asia)

✪ President who was physically handicapped as a result of contracting polio when he was young (Franklin D. Roosevelt)

♦ Most of America's raisins are produced in this state. (California)

❀ Wind Cave National Park is located here. (South Dakota)

♣ What are the opening paragraphs of both the Declaration of Independence and the U.S. Constitution called? (Preamble)

✪ He anchored the *CBS Evening News* for many years and he ended every broadcast with ". . .and that's the way it was . . . ." (Walter Cronkite)

♦ The street in Beverly Hills that has become synonymous with elegant shopping (Rodeo Drive)

❀ *John F. Kennedy's policy that dealt with Latin America, a policy that was continued on by Lyndon Johnson when Kennedy was assassinated (Alliance for Progress)

☘ The most active volcano in the United States (Mt. Kilauea in Hawaii)

✪ In what state is Arches National Park located? (Utah)

♦ America's number one commercial fishing state (California)

❀ What is the only flag that can be legally flown above the American flag in the United States? (The flag of the United Nations)

☘ When Henry Hudson sailed up what is now the river that bears his name, he was sailing under the flag of what European country? (Netherlands)

✪ Name the animal that is a part of the logo of the United States Postal Service. (Bald eagle)

♦ America's first billionaire (John D. Rockefeller)

❀ In which state would one go to visit Capitol Reef National Park? (Utah)

☘ More avocados and figs are grown in this state than in any other. (California)

✪ The constitutional amendment that gave women the right to vote (Nineteenth)

♦ This original "King of Rock 'n Roll" was born in Tupelo, Mississippi.(Elvis Presley)

❀ The major U.S. sporting event delayed eleven days by the earthquake of 1989 (World Series)

GA1157

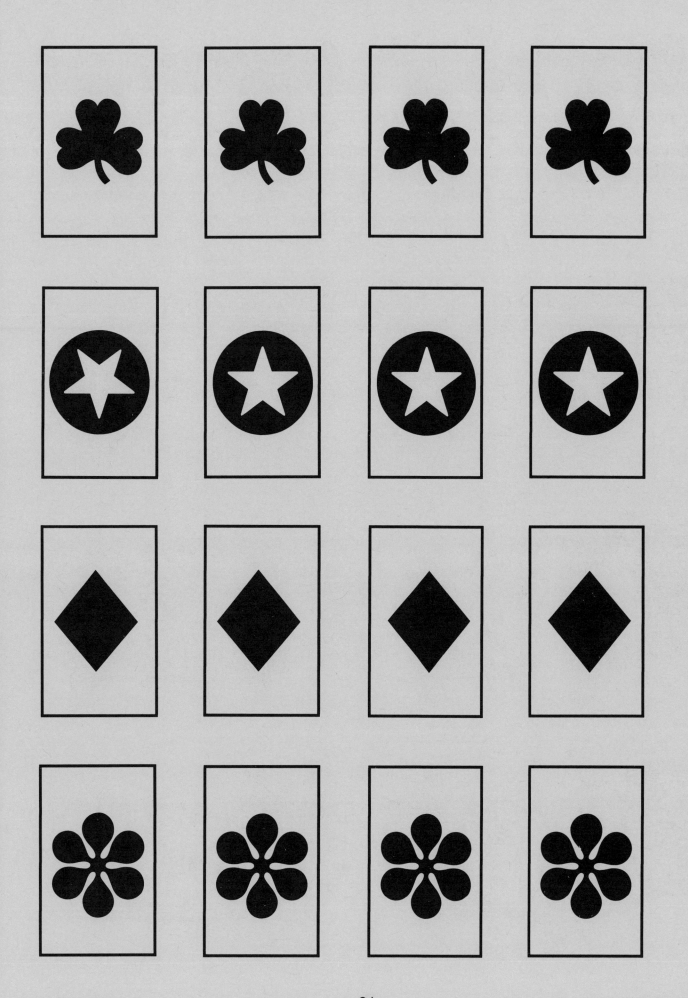

GA1157

92

93

GA1157

94

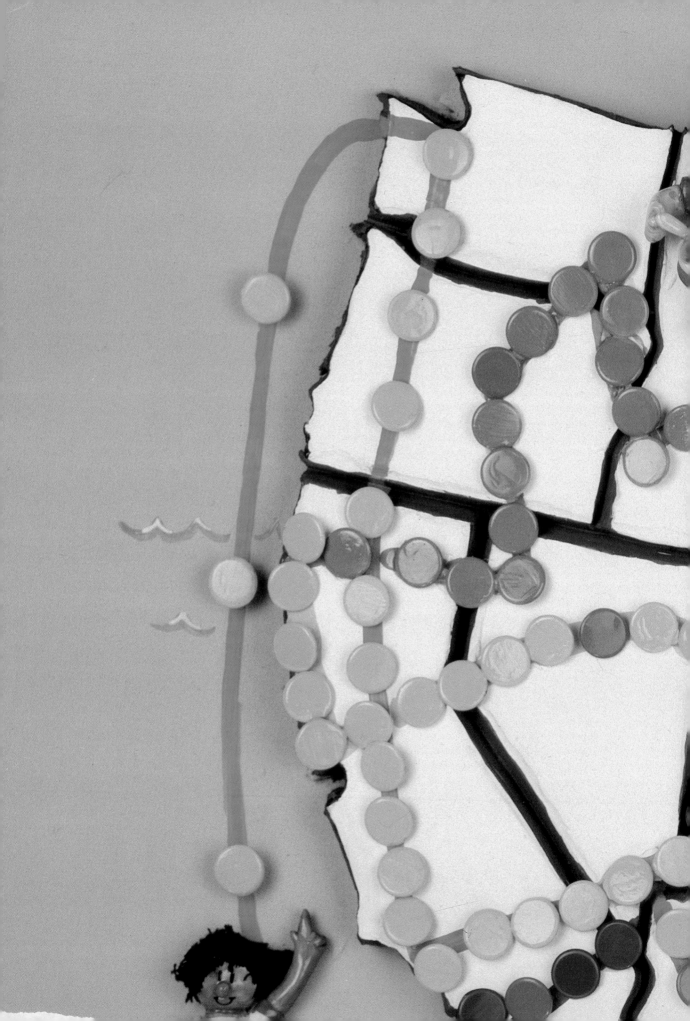

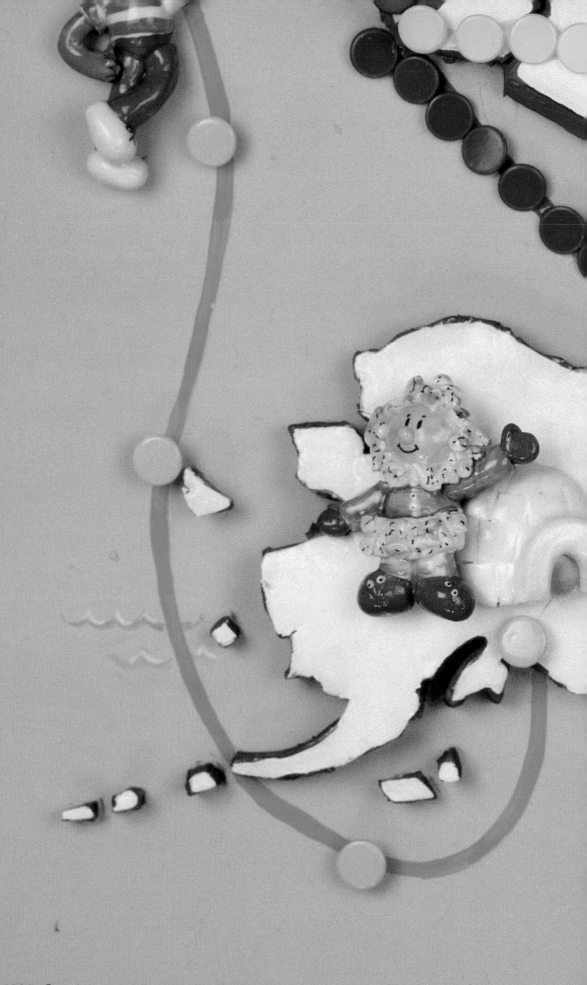